APHASIA REHABILITATION

APHASIA REHABILITATION

An Auditory and Verbal
Task Hierarchy

By

DEBORAH ROSS, M.A., C.C.C. *and* **SARA SPENCER, M.S., C.C.C.**

Speech Pathologists
Department of Physical Medicine and Rehabilitation
Sacramento Medical Center
University of California, Davis
Sacramento, California

CHARLES C THOMAS • PUBLISHER
Springfield • Illinois • U.S.A.

Published and Distributed Throughout the World by
CHARLES C THOMAS • PUBLISHER
Bannerstone House
301-327 East Lawrence Avenue, Springfield, Illinois, U.S.A.

© 1980, *by* CHARLES C THOMAS • PUBLISHER

ISBN 0-398-04031-1 (cloth)
ISBN 0-398-04024-9 (paper)
Library of Congress Catalog Card Number: 79-24617

*With THOMAS BOOKS careful attention is given to all details of manufacturing and design.
It is the Publisher's desire to present books that are satisfactory as to their physical qualities
and artistic possibilities and appropriate for their particular use. THOMAS BOOKS will be
true to those laws of quality that assure a good name and good will.*

Liobrary of Congress Cataloging in Publication Data

Ross, deborah, 1950-
Aphasia rehabiliation.

Bibliography: p.
1. Aphasia—Rehabilitation. I. Spencer, Sara,
1950- joint author. II. Title.
RC425.R67   616.8'552'06   79-24617
ISBN 0-398-04031-1
ISBN 0-398-04024-9 pbk.

Printed in the United States of America
Wm-11

INTRODUCTION

This clinician's manual for the treatment of the aphasic adult contains a selection of treatment tasks for the two primary communicative modalities—auditory processing and verbal expression. The manual is divided into two major sections (auditory and verbal) with each section containing activities presented in a task hierarchy.

The manual was developed primarily for clinicians' use. It is both extensive and comprehensive in that stimulus material for all levels of aphasic involvement (from marked to mild) is contained within each task hierarchy. It is portable and efficient; a score sheet and all necessary materials are contained within the manual.

Although this manual is written with the aphasic adult in mind, selected tasks are also appropriate for apractic and dysarthric patients and those who are cognitively impaired. Suggestions for specific application are included in each section.

ACKNOWLEDGMENTS

We are greatly indebted to three special persons who contributed to the completion of this project. We are grateful to Susan Slakey and Wendy Walker for their excellent and clear illustrations. We wish to thank Julia Halladay Robinson for her many hours of typing and editing for the completion of this manual.

CONTENTS

APHASIA REHABILITATION

SECTION ONE

AUDITORY PROCESSING

INTRODUCTION
SINGLE UNIT PROCESSING
   Identification of Single Objects Named
   Answering Single Unit Yes-No Questions
TWO UNIT PROCESSING
   Answering Personal Two Unit Yes-No Questions
   Following Two Unit Body Part Commands
   Following Two Unit Commands with Visual Stimuli
   Identification of Objects Described by Function
   Identification of Objects Described by Other Characteristics
   Identification of Two Objects Named Serially
   Answering Two Unit Yes-No Questions
THREE UNIT PROCESSING
   Following Three Unit Body Part Commands
   Following Three Unit Commands with Visual Stimuli
   Identification of Three Objects Named Serially
   Answering Three Unit Yes-No Questions
MULTIPLE UNIT PROCESSING
   Following Multiunit Body Part Commands
   Following Multiunit Commands with Visual Stimuli
   Answering Multiunit Yes-No Questions
   Following Multiunit Commands—*Temporal Relations*
   Following Multiunit Commands—*Spatial Relations*
   Following If-Then Commands with Visual Stimuli
   Following If-Then Body Part Commands
   Answering Multiunit Yes-No Questions—*Comparatives*
   Answering Multiunit Yes-No Questions—*Temporal Relations*
   Answering Multiunit Yes-No Questions—*Spatial Relations*
PARAGRAPH COMPREHENSION
   My Grandmother
   The Oldest Man

Cauliflower
McDonald's Hamburgers
Horseradish
Howard Hughes
Monaco
Nantucket
The Dinner
Michael Malloy

INTRODUCTION

This section of the manual is focused on drills designed to strengthen the auditory processing modality. The treatment tasks developed and selected for this section include:

1. Tasks requiring single unit processing.
   a. Identification of objects named
   b. Answering yes-no questions
2. Tasks requiring two unit processing.
   a. Identification of objects named
   b. Identification of objects described
   c. Following two unit commands
   d. Answering yes-no questions
3. Tasks requiring three unit processing.
   a. Identification of objects named
   b. Following three unit commands
   c. Answering yes-no questions
4. Tasks requiring multiple unit processing.
   a. Answering yes-no questions containing comparatives, temporal relations, spatial relations, and if-then situations
   b. Following multiple unit commands
5. Paragraph comprehension.

These treatment tasks were selected to strengthen auditory processing deficits of retention, sequencing, slow rise time, intermittent auditory imperception, reduced information capacity, noise buildup, and shifting ability. The treatment tasks are presented in a task hierarchy, first introducing single units of information and progressing to multiple units of information, thus strengthening the aphasic adults' potential capacity for processing auditory information.

The following variables were considered when establishing this task hierarchy:

1. *Length of Stimuli.* The number of words in the stimuli, including small functor words as well as the number of substantive units contained in the stimuli, were considered in the stimuli development and placement in the hierarchy.
2. *Semantic complexity of stimuli.* A stimuli's use in the English language was considered an important factor. High frequency words are known to be easier to process than low frequency words.
3. *Syntactic complexity of stimuli.* Treatment tasks were developed and selected with syntactic structures in mind. Such structures include

grammatic contrasts e.g. prepositions "on" vs. "under"; morphemic contrasts, e.g. plurality; word order and properties of words in sentences, e.g. subject vs. object. Additional syntactic structures included in higher level tasks are those which require high level auditory sequencing and retention abilities, e.g. comparatives, before and after constructs, if-then commands, and questions.

4. *Presence or absence of visual cues.* Auditory stimuli accompanied by visual cues are easier to process than auditory stimuli presented without visual cues.

5. *Redundancy of material.* The type and amount of additional auditory cues necessary for eliciting a response.

6. *Relationships between substantive words used in the stimulus.* When the substantive words within a stimulus are related, the stimuli will be more easily processed than when they are unrelated, e.g. "Do you get milk from a cow?" will be an easier task than "Point to *cow* and *spoon*" because the two substantive units in the first example are related and therefore more easily processed.

7. *Rise time.* The patient whose processing system is characterized by slow rise time tends to miss the initial portions of incoming auditory messages because his/her processing system takes a greater amount of time to shift from a passive nonprocessing state to an active processing state. Therefore, development and selection of treatment tasks were selected with this factor in mind.

It is suggested that the clinician also consider what he/she can do to control the task hierarchy. The variables that are clinician controlled include the following:

1. *Speed of delivery.* This variable affects the rise time, shifting abilities, retention, and noise buildup.

2. *Stress produced on substantive words.* This provides for cueing for a response through intonation and stress.

3. *Repetition of stimulus.*

4. *Clinician introduction of additional auditory and/or visual cues.*

The auditory task hierarchy is theoretical and should not be implemented as an absolute sequence of progression for all patients. It is suggested that the clinician proceed in a task hierarchy, however, selecting those treatment tasks which are most appropriate for each individual patient. For example, some patients who experience more difficulty with auditory processing than with verbal expression may find that pointing to two objects named will be an easier task than answering a two unit yes-no question and vice versa. Another patient may respond better to tasks with visual cues, though the stimulus contains two unrelated words while another may respond best to the yes-no questions because of contextual cues.

It should be noted that some tasks in this section are particularily applicable to the cognitively impaired patient. All of the higher level auditory tasks are beneficial due to the frequent problems in auditory sequencing and retention abilities in this population. The temporal relations and spatial relation tasks, however, we have found to be particularily useful therapy material.

SINGLE UNIT PROCESSING

IDENTIFICATION OF SINGLE OBJECTS NAMED

MATERIALS: A Pictures, B Pictures, and C Pictures.

TASK INSTRUCTIONS: Arrange the stimulus items in two rows of five (A Pictures).

CLINICIAN INSTRUCTIONS: "I'll say the name of each picture, and you point to it."
If ten stimulus items are too many initially, reduce the number of stimulus items according to the patient's ability and proceed with the activity as directed.

SUGGESTED CRITERIA FOR ADVANCING TO B AND C PICTURES: 100 percent accuracy without the need of repetition of the task instructions or significant delays in responding.

POINT TO THE—

A PICTURES	*B PICTURES*	*C PICTURES*
1. cup	1. bell	1. calendar
2. phone	2. saw	2. parachute
3. spoon	3. pipe	3. battery
4. car	4. tent	4. lawnmower
5. chair	5. radio	5. envelope
6. brush	6. umbrella	6. helicopter
7. watch	7. saddle	7. camera
8. money	8. kite	8. stapler
9. bed	9. flashlight	9. fire hydrant
10. book	10. refrigerator	10. scale

ANSWERING SINGLE UNIT YES-NO QUESTIONS

MATERIALS: None.

TASK INSTRUCTIONS: Ask the patient questions without the presence of the visual stimuli.

CLINICIAN INSTRUCTIONS: "I'm going to ask you some questions, and I want you to answer/indicate yes or no."

SUGGESTED CRITERIA: 90 percent accuracy without the need of repetition of the task instructions or significant delays in responding.

1. Are you a man?
2. Are you asleep?
3. Are you married?
4. Are you hungry?
5. Do you have a cold?
6. Are you thin?
7. Are you tired?
8. Are you tall?
9. Are you in a hospital?
10. Do you wear makeup?
11. Do you have a beard?
12. Do you have hands?
13. Do you have a wife?
14. Do you shave?
15. Are you angry?
16. Do you have a nose?
17. Are you bald?
18. Are you dressed?
19. Are you awake?
20. Do you have legs?

TWO UNIT PROCESSING

ANSWERING PERSONAL TWO UNIT YES-NO QUESTIONS

MATERIALS:	None.
TASK INSTRUCTIONS:	Ask the patient questions without the presence of visual stimuli.
CLINICIAN INSTRUCTIONS:	"I'm going to ask you some questions, and I want you to answer/indicate yes or no."
SUGGESTED CRITERIA:	90 percent accuracy without the need of repetition of the task instructions or significant delays in responding.

1. Are you wearing a skirt?
2. Do you have blue eyes?
3. Do you have a brother?
4. Are you wearing a belt?
5. Do you have shoes on?
6. Do you live alone?
7. Do you have long hair?
8. Do you wear dentures?
9. Do you have two children?
10. Do you live in California?
11. Are you wearing pants?
12. Do you have a ring on?
13. Are you wearing a necklace?
14. Are you wearing a watch?
15. Are your hands dirty?
16. Are you wearing a bathrobe?
17. Are your socks/shoes blue?
18. Do you have red hair?
19. Are your fingernails long?
20. Have you eaten lunch?

ANSWERING PERSONAL TWO UNIT YES-NO QUESTIONS

MATERIALS:	None
TASK INSTRUCTIONS:	Ask the patient questions without the presence of visual stimuli.
CLINICIAN INSTRUCTIONS:	"I'm going to ask you some questions, and I want you to answer/indicate yes or no."
SUGGESTED CRITERIA:	90 percent accuracy without the need of repetition of the task instructions or significant delays in responding.

1. Do you have curly hair?
2. Do you have a jacket on?
3. Do you wear eyeglasses?
4. Do you have a broken finger?
5. Do you watch T.V.?
6. Are your hands cold?
7. Do you listen to music?
8. Do you have ten fingers?
9. Do you live in New York?
10. Is your hair grey?
11. Are your fingernails painted?
12. Are your ears pierced?
13. Do you have a roommate?
14. Are you a black man/woman?
15. Do you have two feet?
16. Are you a good cook?
17. Do you have three legs?
18. Are you right-handed?
19. Do you like chocolate?
20. Is your nose bleeding?

FOLLOWING TWO UNIT BODY PART COMMANDS

MATERIALS: None.

TASK INSTRUCTIONS: None.

CLINICIAN INSTRUCTIONS: "I'm going to have you do some things with certain parts of your body. Listen carefully and do just what I tell you to do."

SUGGESTED CRITERIA: 90 percent accuracy without the need of repetition of the task instructions or significant delays in responding.

1. Touch your nose.
2. Raise your hand.
3. Wink at me.
4. Bend your thumb.
5. Point to me.
6. Close your eyes.
7. Open your mouth.
8. Smile at me.
9. Turn away.
10. Wrinkle your nose.
11. Shake your head.
12. Lift your foot.
13. Frown at me.
14. Scratch your head.
15. Bend your knee.
16. Point to your ear.
17. Show me your teeth.
18. Pucker your lips.
19. Wiggle your toes.
20. Scratch your arm.

FOLLOWING TWO UNIT BODY PART COMMANDS

MATERIALS: None.

TASK INSTRUCTIONS: None.

CLINICIAN INSTRUCTIONS: "I'm going to have you do some things with certain parts of your body. Listen carefully and do just what I tell you to do."

SUGGESTED CRITERIA: 90 percent accuracy without the need of repetition of the task instructions or significant delays in responding.

 1. Stick out your tongue.
 2. Wag your finger.
 3. Twist your head.
 4. Shrug your shoulders.
 5. Touch your knee.
 6. Pull your hair.
 7. Blink twice.
 8. Clap your hands.
 9. Look at my hair.
10. Lick your lips.
11. Look around.
12. Make a face.
13. Wiggle your thumb.
14. Lift your eyebrow.
15. Touch your chin.
16. Pat your head.
17. Show me your neck.
18. Shake my hand.
19. Touch my elbow.
20. Pull at your ear.

FOLLOWING TWO UNIT COMMANDS WITH VISUAL STIMULI

MATERIALS: A Pictures.

TASK INSTRUCTIONS: Arrange the stimulus items in two rows of five.

CLINICIAN INSTRUCTIONS: "I'm going to have you do some things with each of these. Listen carefully and do just what I tell you to do."

SUGGESTED CRITERIA: 90 percent accuracy without the need of repetition of the task instructions or significant delays in responding.

1. Turn over the cup.
2. Pick up the chair.
3. Give me the phone.
4. Point to the spoon.
5. Touch the book.
6. Pick up the money.
7. Turn over the watch.
8. Point to the brush.
9. Give me the chair.
10. Touch the car.
11. Look at the bed.
12. Push away the money.
13. Give me the watch.
14. Point to the brush.
15. Turn over the spoon.
16. Touch the phone.
17. Give me the money.
18. Pick up the book.
19. Push away the brush.
20. Turn over the car.

FOLLOWING TWO UNIT COMMANDS WITH VISUAL STIMULI

MATERIALS:	B Pictures.
TASK INSTRUCTIONS:	Arrange the stimulus items in two rows of five.
CLINICIAN INSTRUCTIONS:	"I'm going to have you do some things with each of these. Listen carefully and do just what I tell you to do."
SUGGESTED CRITERIA:	90 percent accuracy without the need of repetition of the task instructions or significant delays in responding.

1. Turn over the saw.
2. Pick up the tent.
3. Point to the radio.
4. Give me the kite.
5. Push away the pipe.
6. Touch the bell.
7. Pick up the saw.
8. Point to the umbrella.
9. Turn over the saddle.
10. Give me the pipe.
11. Push away the flashlight.
12. Touch the saw.
13. Pick up the bell.
14. Point to the tent.
15. Give me the radio.
16. Turn over the refrigerator.
17. Push away the kite.
18. Touch the pipe.
19. Pick up the bell.
20. Point to the saddle.

FOLLOWING TWO UNIT COMMANDS WITH VISUAL STIMULI

MATERIALS:	C Pictures.
TASK INSTRUCTIONS:	Arrange the stimulus items in two rows of five.
CLINICIAN INSTRUCTIONS:	"I'm going to have you do some things with each of these. Listen carefully and do just what I tell you to do."
SUGGESTED CRITERIA:	90 percent accuracy without the need of repetition of the task instructions or significant delays in responding.

1. Turn over the calendar.
2. Pick up the lawn mower.
3. Point to the helicopter.
4. Give me the fire hydrant.
5. Push away the stapler.
6. Touch the battery.
7. Pick up the camera.
8. Point to the scale.
9. Turn over the parachute.
10. Give me the envelope.
11. Push away the battery.
12. Touch the lawn mower.
13. Pick up the calendar.
14. Point to the helicopter.
15. Touch the fire hydrant.
16. Turn over the stapler.
17. Push away the camera.
18. Touch the scale.
19. Pick up the parachute.
20. Point to the envelope.

IDENTIFICATION OF OBJECTS DESCRIBED BY FUNCTION

MATERIALS: A Pictures.

TASK INSTRUCTIONS: Arrange the stimulus items in
                              two rows of five.

CLINICIAN INSTRUCTIONS: "I'll describe each picture, and
                              you point to it."

SUGGESTED CRITERIA: 90 percent accuracy without the
                              need of repetition of the task
                              instructions or significant delays
                              in responding.

POINT TO THE ONE USED FOR—
1. telling time.
2. sleeping in.
3. driving.
4. fixing hair.
5. buying things.
6. calling people.
7. reading.
8. drinking.
9. stirring.
10. sitting in.

IDENTIFICATION OF OBJECTS DESCRIBED BY FUNCTION

MATERIALS:	B Pictures.
TASK INSTRUCTIONS:	Arrange the stimulus items in two rows of five.
CLINICIAN INSTRUCTIONS:	"I'll describe each picture, and you point to it."
SUGGESTED CRITERIA:	90 percent accuracy without the need of repetition of the task instructions or significant delays in responding.

POINT TO THE ONE USED FOR—
1. smoking.
2. cutting wood.
3. riding on a horse.
4. keeping food cold.
5. listening to music.
6. seeing in the dark.
7. ringing.
8. walking in the rain.
9. flying in the wind.
10. sleeping in the woods.

IDENTIFICATION OF OBJECTS DESCRIBED BY FUNCTION

MATERIALS: C Pictures.

TASK INSTRUCTIONS: Arrange the stimulus items in two rows of five.

CLINICIAN INSTRUCTIONS: "I'll describe each picture, and you point to it."

SUGGESTED CRITERIA: 90 percent accuracy without the need of repetition of the task instruction or significant delays in responding.

POINT TO THE ONE—
1. you use to find the date.
2. that makes a flashlight run.
3. you take pictures with.
4. that you put a letter in.
5. that you cut the lawn with.
6. that you put two pieces of paper together with.
7. that you can fly in.
8. that provides water for firemen.
9. that you weigh yourself with.
10. that you jump out of a plane with.

IDENTIFICATION OF OBJECTS DESCRIBED BY OTHER CHARACTERISTICS

MATERIALS:	A Pictures.
TASK INSTRUCTIONS:	Arrange the stimulus items in two rows of five.
CLINICIAN INSTRUCTIONS:	"I'll describe each picture, and you point to it."
SUGGESTED CRITERIA:	90 percent accuracy without the need of repetition of the task instructions or significant delays in responding.

POINT TO THE ONE THAT—
1. has bristles and a handle.
2. has four wheels on it.
3. has paper in it.
4. has a dial and a cord.
5. has sheets and a pillow.
6. you can wear around your wrist.
7. has four legs.
8. you put in a wallet.
9. ticks, and you wind it.
10. is made of metal and has a handle.

IDENTIFICATION OF OBJECTS DESCRIBED BY OTHER CHARACTERISTICS

MATERIALS: B Pictures.

TASK INSTRUCTIONS: Arrange the stimulus items in two rows of five.

CLINICIAN INSTRUCTIONS: "I'll describe each picture, and you point to it."

SUGGESTED CRITERIA: 90 percent accuracy without the need of repetition of the task instructions or significant delays in responding.

POINT TO THE ONE THAT—
1. has knobs and plays music.
2. is made of leather and has stirrups.
3. you find in a kitchen.
4. you put tobacco in.
5. you set up in the woods.
6. has a sharp serrated edge.
7. is diamond shaped.
8. is small and has a light bulb.
9. has a handle and is round at the bottom.
10. opens up over your head.

IDENTIFICATION OF OBJECTS DESCRIBED BY OTHER CHARACTERISTICS

MATERIALS: C Pictures.

TASK INSTRUCTIONS: Arrange the stimulus items in two rows of five.

CLINICIAN INSTRUCTIONS: "I'll describe each picture, and you point to it."

SUGGESTED CRITERIA: 90 percent accuracy without the need of repetition of the task instructions or significant delays in responding.

POINT TO THE ONE—
1. that hangs on a wall.
2. that you find in a bathroom.
3. that has sharp blades in it.
4. that you find on a sidewalk.
5. that you put film in.
6. that is white and rectangular.
7. that opens up in the sky.
8. that has propellers on it.
9. that has twelve months on it.
10. that is small and cylindrical.

IDENTIFICATION OF TWO OBJECTS NAMED SERIALLY

MATERIALS:	A Pictures.
TASK INSTRUCTIONS:	Arrange the stimulus items in two rows of five.
CLINICIAN INSTRUCTIONS:	"I'll say the name of two objects, and you point to them in the order that I say them."
SUGGESTED CRITERIA:	90 percent accuracy without the need of repetition of the task instructions or significant delays in responding.

POINT TO THE—
1. phone and chair.
2. book and watch.
3. spoon and cup.
4. brush and money.
5. car and bed.
6. chair and watch.
7. book and phone.
8. cup and money.
9. brush and spoon.
10. car and chair.
11. bed and watch.
12. book and cup.
13. money and phone.
14. brush and car.
15. chair and cup.
16. watch and phone.
17. spoon and money.
18. bed and book.
19. phone and brush.
20. spoon and chair.

IDENTIFICATION OF TWO OBJECTS NAMED SERIALLY

MATERIALS: B Pictures.

TASK INSTRUCTIONS: Arrange the stimulus items in two rows of five.

CLINICIAN INSTRUCTIONS: "I'll say the name of two objects, and you point to them in the order that I say them."

SUGGESTED CRITERIA: 90 percent accuracy without the need of repetition of the task instructions or significant delays in responding.

POINT TO THE—

1. radio and pipe.
2. tent and bell.
3. flashlight and saw.
4. refrigerator and saddle.
5. umbrella and kite.
6. radio and tent.
7. pipe and bell.
8. saw and saddle.
9. kite and tent.
10. radio and umbrella.
11. flashlight and saw.
12. pipe and bell.
13. tent and pipe.
14. refrigerator and pipe.
15. saw and kite.
16. umbrella and bell.
17. saddle and tent.
18. saddle and flashlight.
19. kite and umbrella.
20. flashlight and refrigerator.

IDENTIFICATION OF TWO OBJECTS NAMED SERIALLY

MATERIALS:	C Pictures.
TASK INSTRUCTIONS:	Arrange the stimulus items in two rows of five.
CLINICIAN INSTRUCTIONS:	"I'll say the name of two objects, and you point to them in the order that I say them."
SUGGESTED CRITERIA:	90 percent accuracy without the need of repetition of the task instructions or significant delays in responding.

POINT TO THE—
1. calendar and parachute.
2. scale and envelope.
3. lawn mower and battery.
4. stapler and fire hydrant.
5. helicopter and camera.
6. calendar and scale.
7. parachute and envelope.
8. lawn mower and stapler.
9. parachute and fire hydrant.
10. helicopter and battery.
11. camera and scale.
12. envelope and stapler.
13. battery and camera.
14. fire hydrant and helicopter.
15. scale and parachute.
16. calendar and envelope.
17. stapler and camera.
18. battery and fire hydrant.
19. parachute and lawn mower.
20. envelope and scale.

ANSWERING TWO UNIT YES-NO QUESTIONS

MATERIALS: None.

TASK INSTRUCTIONS: Ask the patient questions without the presence of the visual stimuli.

CLINICIAN INSTRUCTIONS: "I'm going to ask you some questions, and I want you to answer/indicate yes or no."

SUGGESTED CRITERIA: 90 percent accuracy without the need of repetition of the task instructions or significant delays in responding.

1. Do birds have wings?
2. Do girls wear beards?
3. Is it ten o'clock?
4. Is my sister a girl?
5. Do you see with your tongue?
6. Does ice feel cold?
7. Do fish have feet?
8. Does a cat have feathers?
9. Do children go to school?
10. Do cars have wings?
11. Do puppies have ears?
12. Does a kite have a motor?
13. Do eagles have feathers?
14. Do you swim in the snow?
15. Do you measure with a ruler?
16. Is a piano an instrument?
17. Do you cut with a crayon?
18. Do you see with your eyes?
19. Do you have toes on your feet?
20. Do you sleep on a table?

ANSWERING TWO UNIT YES-NO QUESTIONS

MATERIALS:	None.
TASK INSTRUCTIONS:	Ask the patient questions without the presence of the visual stimuli.
CLINICIANS INSTRUCTIONS:	"I'm going to ask you some questions, and I want you to answer/indicate yes or no."
SUGGESTED CRITERIA:	90 percent accuracy without the need of repetition of the task instructions or significant delays in responding.

1. Do kitchens have sinks?
2. Is a tree an animal?
3. Can you ride on a horse?
4. Is a window on the floor?
5. Does a briefcase have a handle?
6. Do pianos have keys?
7. Do you climb a book?
8. Is your mother a man?
9. Do you eat food?
10. Do books have pages?
11. Does a dog laugh?
12. Can you chew gum?
13. Do boys wear shirts?
14. Do you shave with a saw?
15. Do you eat with a fork?
16. Do you type on a television?
17. Do trees have bark?
18. Do you wash with soap?
19. Do bathrooms have stoves?
20. Are measles something to drink?

ANSWERING TWO UNIT YES-NO QUESTIONS

MATERIALS: None.

TASK INSTRUCTIONS: Ask the patient questions without the presence of the visual stimuli.

CLINICIAN INSTRUCTIONS: "I'm going to ask you some questions, and I want you to answer/indicate yes or no."

SUGGESTED CRITERIA: 90 percent accuracy without the need of repetition of the task instructions or significant delays in responding.

1. Do cows sing?
2. Do ducks swim?
3. Are babies tall?
4. Does hair grow?
5. Do birds fly?
6. Is fire hot?
7. Do houses walk?
8. Do children drive?
9. Do dogs meow?
10. Do doors open?
11. Is glue sticky?
12. Do scissors cut?
13. Is candy Sweet?
14. Do books write?
15. Do trees grow?
16. Do boys play?
17. Do balls bounce?
18. Is summer hot?
19. Do boxes wiggle?
20. Do pencils talk?

ANSWERING TWO UNIT YES-NO QUESTIONS

MATERIALS:	None.
TASK INSTRUCTIONS:	Ask the patient questions without the presence of the visual stimuli.
CLINICIAN INSTRUCTIONS:	"I'm going to ask you some questions, and I want you to answer/indicate yes or no."
SUGGESTED CRITERIA:	90 percent accuracy without the need of repetition of the task instructions or significant delays in responding.

1. Are blankets warm?
2. Do cats bark?
3. Do windows close?
4. Are marbles square?
5. Are witches ugly?
6. Does wood float?
7. Do watches sing?
8. Does the moon shine?
9. Is fur soft?
10. Are fires cool?
11. Is mud dirty?
12. Do boats swim?
13. Do people cry?
14. Do candles melt?
15. Do planes walk?
16. Do the blind see?
17. Do watches tick?
18. Does a rooster crow?
19. Are apples blue?
20. Is rain wet?

ANSWERING TWO UNIT YES-NO QUESTIONS

MATERIALS:	None.
TASK INSTRUCTIONS:	Ask the patient questions without the presence of the visual stimuli.
CLINICIAN INSTRUCTIONS:	"I'm going to ask you some questions, and I want you to answer/indicate yes or no."
SUGGESTED CRITERIA:	90 percent accuracy without the need of repetition of the task instructions or significant delays in responding.

1. Are eggs oval?
2. Do frogs leap?
3. Are boys female?
4. Do kings rule?
5. Are envelopes rectangular?
6. Do you eat tables?
7. Are lemons sweet?
8. Are lightbulbs bright?
9. Are scissors sharp?
10. Is milk green?
11. Are elephants big?
12. Do chickens dance?
13. Are needles sharp?
14. Is sugar sour?
15. Are doors round?
16. Are ants small?
17. Do phones ring?
18. Is popcorn alive?
19. Can paper burn?
20. Does glass break?

THREE UNIT PROCESSING

FOLLOWING THREE UNIT BODY PART COMMANDS

MATERIALS: None.

TASK INSTRUCTIONS: Ask the patient questions without the presence of the visual stimuli.

CLINICIAN INSTRUCTIONS: "I'm going to ask you to do certain things with parts of your body. Listen carefully and do just what I tell you to do."

SUGGESTED CRITERIA: 90 percent accuracy without the need of repetition of the task instructions or significant delays in responding.

1. Blink your eyes twice.
2. Point to me and smile.
3. Scratch your head with two fingers.
4. Tap your shoulder twice.
5. Nod your head towards the wall.
6. Touch your nose and mouth.
7. Smile and shake your finger.
8. Touch your nose and wink.
9. Shrug your shoulders and nod.
10. Pull your ear twice.
11. Bend your left arm.
12. Point your toe at the wall.
13. Shut your eyes tightly.
14. Smile and rub your hands.
15. Raise your left hand.
16. Scratch your chin and squint.
17. Lift both hands.
18. Pull at your right ear.
19. Straighten out your left arm.
20. Scratch your shoulder and your ear.

FOLLOWING THREE UNIT BODY PART COMMANDS

MATERIALS:	None.
TASK INSTRUCTIONS:	Ask the patient questions without the presence of the visual stimuli.
CLINICIAN INSTRUCTIONS:	"Im going to ask you to do certain things with parts of your body. Listen carefully and do just what I tell you to do."
SUGGESTED CRITERIA:	90 percent accuracy without the need of repetition of the task instructions or significant delays in responding.

1. Point to your knee and your elbow.
2. Scratch your chin and wink.
3. Smile and rub your forehead.
4. Touch your chin and your wrist.
5. Raise your eyebrows twice.
6. Bend your left thumb.
7. Straighten your knee and nod.
8. Rub the palms of your hands.
9. Touch your shoulder with your chin.
10. Touch your eyebrow and your chin.
11. Wrinkle your forehead and blink.
12. Raise your elbow and your chin.
13. Bend your wrist and your thumb.
14. Smile and point to your waist.
15. Look at your foot and wiggle it.
16. Put your thumbs together.
17. Put your hand under your chin.
18. Raise your elbow twice.
19. Touch your left knee.
20. Place your wrists together.

FOLLOWING THREE UNIT COMMANDS WITH VISUAL STIMULI

MATERIALS: A Pictures.

TASK INSTRUCTIONS: Arrange stimulus items in two rows of five.

CLINICIAN INSTRUCTIONS: "I'm going to have you do some things with each of these. Listen carefully and do just what I tell you to do."

SUGGESTED CRITERIA: 90 percent accuracy without the need of repetition of the task instructions or significant delays in responding.

1. Put the chair in the corner.
2. Turn over the phone and the car.
3. Pick up the watch and the cup.
4. Touch the bed and the brush.
5. Turn over the money and the book.
6. Point to the chair and the phone.
7. Give me the car and the cup.
8. Put the spoon in the corner.
9. Pick up the chair and the brush.
10. Touch the book and the watch.
11. Turn over the spoon and the phone.
12. Give me the bed and the money.
13. Point to the chair and the car.
14. Put the phone in the corner.
15. Turn over the watch and the brush.
16. Give me the spoon and the cup.
17. Point to the chair and the phone.
18. Put the bed in the corner.
19. Pick up the watch and the car.
20. Push away the cup and the money.

FOLLOWING THREE UNIT COMMANDS WITH VISUAL STIMULI

MATERIALS: B Pictures.

TASK INSTRUCTIONS: Arrange stimulus items in two rows of five.

CLINICIAN INSTRUCTIONS: "I'm going to have you do some things with each of these. Listen carefully, and do just what I tell you to do."

SUGGESTED CRITERIA: 90 percent accuracy without the need of repetition of the task instructions or significant delays in responding.

1. Put the bell in the corner.
2. Turn over the radio and the umbrella.
3. Touch the kite and the saw.
4. Pick up the pipe and the tent.
5. Give me the refrigerator and the saddle.
6. Point to the flashlight and the bell.
7. Put the radio in the corner.
8. Turn over the umbrella and the kite.
9. Pick up the saw and the tent.
10. Point to the pipe and the refrigerator.
11. Give me the saddle and the flashlight.
12. Touch the bell and the radio.
13. Put the umbrella in the corner.
14. Pick up the saw and the kite.
15. Turn over the pipe and the tent.
16. Give me the refrigerator and the bell.
17. Touch the flashlight and the bell.
18. Put the kite in the corner.
19. Pick up the saw and the umbrella.
20. Turn over the tent and the pipe.

FOLLOWING THREE UNIT COMMANDS WITH VISUAL STIMULI

MATERIALS: C Pictures.

TASK INSTRUCTIONS: Arrange stimulus items in two rows of five.

CLINICIAN INSTRUCTIONS: "I'm going to have you do some things with each of these. Listen carefully and do just what I tell you to do."

SUGGESTED CRITERIA: 90 percent accuracy without the need of repetition of the task instructions or significant delays in responding.

1. Pick up the battery and the envelope.
2. Put the parachute in the corner.
3. Turn over the calendar and the lawn mower.
4. Give me the fire hydrant and the helicopter.
5. Touch the scale and the camera.
6. Put the stapler in the corner.
7. Pick up the battery and the calendar.
8. Point to the lawn mower and the envelope.
9. Turn over the parachute and the fire hydrant.
10. Give me the helicopter and the camera.
11. Touch the scale and the stapler.
12. Put the battery in the corner.
13. Point to the envelope and the parachute.
14. Turn over the fire hydrant and the helicopter.
15. Touch the camera and the lawn mower.
16. Give me the scale and the calendar.
17. Put the parachute in the corner.
18. Pick up the envelope and the camera.
19. Turn over the scale and the battery.
20. Touch the lawn mower and the calendar.

IDENTIFICATION OF THREE OBJECTS NAMED SERIALLY

MATERIALS: A Pictures.

TASK INSTRUCTIONS: Arrange the stimulus items in
                               two rows of five.

CLINICIAN INSTRUCTIONS: "I'll say the name of three
                               pictures, and you point to them
                               in the order that I say them."

SUGGESTED CRITERIA: 90 percent accuracy without the
                               need of repetition of the task
                               instructions or significant delays
                               in responding.

POINT TO THE—
1. brush, book, and car.
2. money, watch, and cup.
3. bed, chair, and spoon.
4. phone, brush, and car.
5. bed, money, and book.
6. chair, watch, and cup.
7. spoon, brush, and phone.
8. book, chair, and car.
9. bed, cup, and money.
10. phone, watch, and book.
11. chair, spoon, and car.
12. cup, money, and brush.
13. watch, car, and bed.
14. brush, spoon, and phone.
15. book, cup, and money.
16. car, chair, and watch.
17. money, brush, and spoon.
18. phone, book, and watch.
19. cup, spoon, and car.
20. money, chair, and bed.

IDENTIFICATION OF THREE OBJECTS NAMED SERIALLY

MATERIALS: B Pictures.

TASK INSTRUCTIONS: Arrange the stimulus items in
                            two rows of five.

CLINICIAN INSTRUCTIONS: "I'll say the name of three
                            pictures, and you point to them
                            in the order that I say them."

SUGGESTED CRITERIA: 90 percent accuracy without the
                            need of repetition of the task
                            instructions or significant delays
                            in responding.

POINT TO THE—
 1. radio, umbrella, and tent.
 2. kite, saw, and refrigerator.
 3. flashlight, saddle, and pipe.
 4. bell, radio, and tent.
 5. umbrella, saw, and saddle.
 6. tent, refrigerator, and pipe.
 7. radio, kite, and flashlight.
 8. saw, umbrella, and saddle.
 9. refrigerator, kite, and tent.
10. saddle, radio, and pipe.
11. bell, umbrella, and flashlight.
12. kite, saw, and refrigerator.
13. radio, tent, and saddle.
14. pipe, flashlight, and umbrella.
15. bell, refrigerator, and radio.
16. saw, tent, and kite.
17. saddle, umbrella, and pipe.
18. refrigerator, flashlight, and bell.
19. tent, kite, and radio.
20. kite, saw, and pipe.

IDENTIFICATION OF THREE OBJECTS NAMED SERIALLY

MATERIALS:	C Pictures.
TASK INSTRUCTIONS:	Arrange the stimulus items in two rows of five.
CLINICIAN INSTRUCTIONS:	"I'll say the name of three pictures, and you point to them in the order that I say them."
SUGGESTED CRITERIA:	90 percent accuracy without the need of repetition of the task instructions or significant delays in responding.

POINT TO THE—
1. calendar, envelope, and battery.
2. parachute, lawn mower, and scale.
3. helicopter, camera, and fire hydrant.
4. stapler, calendar, and battery.
5. envelope, scale, and parachute.
6. lawn mower, fire hydrant, and helicopter.
7. camera, battery, and stapler.
8. calendar, parachute, and envelope.
9. scale, helicopter, and lawn mower.
10. fire hydrant, stapler, and camera.
11. battery, envelope, and calendar.
12. parachute, camera, and fire hydrant.
13. helicopter, battery, and stapler.
14. envelope, calendar, and camera.
15. scale, lawn mower, and parachute.
16. camera, fire hydrant, and helicopter.
17. stapler, battery, and envelope.
18. calendar, camera, and scale.
19. lawn mower, parachute, and fire hydrant.
20. helicopter, stapler, and battery.

ANSWERING THREE UNIT YES-NO QUESTIONS

MATERIALS: None.

TASK INSTRUCTIONS: Ask the patient questions without the presence of the visual stimuli.

CLINICIAN INSTRUCTIONS: "I'm going to ask you some questions, and I want you to answer/indicate yes or no."

SUGGESTED CRITERIA: 90 percent accuracy without the need of repetition of the task instructions or significant delays in responding.

1. Do you get coffee from a cow?
2. Are windows made of glass?
3. Do you eat breakfast at night?
4. Do you hear with your ears?
5. Do postmen deliver letters?
6. Do you pick up food with a shovel?
7. Do you get wool from a lamb?
8. Do firemen use ladders?
9. Does the sun shine at night?
10. Do barbers cut hair?
11. Does a dog say meow?
12. Do you use a shovel to dig in the ground?
13. Does a boy wear a dress?
14. Is bread always fresh?
15. Do waitresses serve food?
16. Do clowns make people laugh?
17. Do you take snakes for a walk?
18. Do watches tell time?
19. Do you kick a ball with your foot?
20. Is coffee always hot?

ANSWERING THREE UNIT YES-NO QUESTIONS

MATERIALS: None.

TASK INSTRUCTIONS: Ask the patient questions
                              without the presence of the
                              visual stimuli.

CLINICIAN INSTRUCTIONS: "I'm going to ask you some
                              questions, and I want you to
                              answer/indicate yes or no."

SUGGESTED CRITERIA: 90 percent accuracy without the
                              need of repetition of the task
                              instructions or significant delays
                              in responding.

1. Do butchers cut bread?
2. Does a cow drink milk?
3. Does a red light mean stop?
4. Do birds fly in the sky?
5. Do bicycles have four wheels?
6. Do Indians live in teepees?
7. Do dentists fix teeth?
8. Are bricks made of wax?
9. Do musicians play instruments?
10. Is vanilla ice cream black?
11. Do birds like taking baths?
12. Do elephants have long noses?
13. Do you have twelve fingers on your hand?
14. At the zoo, are people in cages?
15. Do hairdressers fix hair?
16. Do carpenters build houses?
17. Are all clocks electric?
18. Do you buy food in a barber shop?
19. Does a hat cover your head?
20. Do stewardesses serve food?

ANSWERING THREE UNIT YES-NO QUESTIONS

MATERIALS: None.

TASK INSTRUCTIONS: Ask the patient questions without the presence of the visual stimuli.

CLINICIAN INSTRUCTIONS: "I'm going to ask you some questions, and I want you to answer/indicate yes or no."

SUGGESTED CRITERIA: 90 percent accuracy without the need of repetition of the task instructions or significant delays in responding.

1. Are anchors made of wood?
2. Are crowded rooms stuffy?
3. Do deliverymen put out fires?
4. Do you lock doors with keys?
5. Do four-legged animals talk?
6. Can you cut a tree with scissors?
7. Does a nurse take your temperature?
8. Do pianos sing songs?
9. Do farmers raise animals?
10. Are soldiers sent to war?
11. Do cows chew milk?
12. Do you wear shoes on your hands?
13. Do you clean grass with a vacuum cleaner?
14. Do dogs wag their tails?
15. Are stoves always hot?
16. Do you put tobacco in a pipe?
17. Does a calendar tell you the date?
18. Do you put a saddle on a pig?
19. Can you cut wood with a saw?
20. Can you boil water in a kettle?

ANSWERING THREE UNIT YES-NO QUESTIONS

MATERIALS:	None.
TASK INSTRUCTIONS:	Ask the patient questions without the presence of the visual stimuli.
CLINICIAN INSTRUCTIONS:	"I'm going to ask you some questions, and I want you to answer/indicate yes or no."
SUGGESTED CRITERIA:	90 percent accuracy without the need of repetition of the task instructions or significant delays in responding.

1. Do you destroy money in a bank?
2. Do lawyers go to court?
3. Do you wear a bracelet on your ankle?
4. Can you cut a bottle with a knife?
5. Do you pound nails with a hammer?
6. Is coffee good for a baby?
7. Do doctors take care of the sick?
8. Do you burn logs in a fireplace?
9. Do you wax a car with soap?
10. Do mountain climbers use rope?
11. Does a cook stir soup?
12. Do bald men have hair?
13. Is an egg as heavy as a balloon?
14. Do firemen carry hoses?
15. Does ice melt in your hand?
16. Are watermelon seeds plastic?
17. Do gardeners cut grass?
18. Do babies ride bikes?
19. Do kites fly in the sky?
20. Do umbrellas keep you dry?

ANSWERING THREE UNIT YES-NO QUESTIONS

MATERIALS: None.

TASK INSTRUCTIONS: Ask the patient questions without the presence of the visual stimuli.

CLINICIAN INSTRUCTIONS: "I'm going to ask you some questions, and I want you to answer/indicate yes or no."

SUGGESTED CRITERIA: 90 percent accuracy without the need of repetition of the task instructions or significant delays in responding.

1. Do savages live in hotels?
2. Are wrinkled dresses smooth?
3. Are broken watches reliable?
4. Are paper napkins absorbent?
5. Do eagles soar through water?
6. Do carpets cover floors?
7. Do salesmen make transactions?
8. Is a banana a blue fruit?
9. Is curly hair straight?
10. Is coffee an alcoholic drink?
11. Is sour milk tasty?
12. Are waxed floors slippery?
13. Are green bananas ripe?
14. Are meaningless phrases informative?
15. Are unplugged refrigerators cold?
16. Are rich people wealthy?
17. Do athletes participate in sports?
18. Do truck drivers haul merchandise?
19. Are sleeping dogs active?
20. Are angry lions dangerous?

5

MULTIPLE UNIT PROCESSING

FOLLOWING MULTIUNIT BODY PART COMMANDS

MATERIALS: None.

TASK INSTRUCTIONS: None.

CLINICIAN INSTRUCTIONS: "I'm going to have you do some things with certain parts of your body. Listen carefully and do just what I tell you to do."

SUGGESTED CRITERIA: 90 percent accuracy without the need of repetition of the task instructions or significant delays in responding.

 1. Point to me, the ceiling, and the floor.
 2. Close your eyes, raise your hands, and look at me.
 3. Blink twice, and point at me.
 4. Tap your right shoulder with your left hand.
 5. Touch your nose, your wrist, and your thumb.
•6. When I touch my nose, you raise your hand.
 7. Shake your finger, then shrug your shoulders.
 8. When I nod my head, you put your thumbs together.
 9. Touch your left hand with your right index finger.
10. Instead of touching your chin, touch your nose.
11. When I shrug my shoulders, you nod your head.
12. Touch your knee, your elbow, and your chin.
13. Shrug your shoulders, and stomp your left foot.
14. Touch your chin with the back of your left hand.
15. Scratch your head, point to me, then smile.
16. Look at the ceiling instead of nodding your head.
17. Put your left hand under your right hand.
18. Instead of raising your hand, nod your head.
19. Touch your nose and chin instead of clapping your hands.
20. Touch your left thumb with your right index finger.

FOLLOWING MULTIUNIT BODY PART COMMANDS

MATERIALS: None.

TASK INSTRUCTIONS: None.

CLINICIAN INSTRUCTIONS: "I'm going to have you do some things with certain parts of your body. Listen carefully and do just what I tell you to do."

SUGGESTED CRITERIA: 90 percent accuracy without the need of repetition of the task instructions or significant delays in responding.

1. Touch your chin three times with your thumb.
2. Touch your nose, raise your hand, and close your eyes.
3. Look at the ceiling, point to me, and shrug your shoulders.
4. Nod your head two times, keeping your hand on top of it.
5. Put your hand on your shoulder for as long as I put my hand on my shoulder.
6. When I nod my head, you raise your hand and make a fist.
7. Touch your head, your knee, and your neck.
8. Touch the back of your right hand with the back of your left hand.
9. Keep your hand on your head until I count to five.
10. Put your hands together when I say "Now".
11. Touch one ear twice and the other ear once.
12. Close your eyes and point to your elbow and your chin.
13. Put your wrists together when I touch both my shoulders.
14. Put your hand under your chin and wink when I point to you.
15. Touch the one you smell with and the ones you hear with.
16. Put your left hand behind your left ear and shrug your shoulders.
17. Point to the ceiling when I point to the floor, and touch your nose when I nod.
18. Make a fist, raise your hand and touch your forehead.
19. Put your hand on your hip, shrug your shoulders twice, and wrinkle your nose.
20. Touch your chin with the palm of your left hand, and touch your nose with your left index finger.

FOLLOWING MULTIUNIT COMMANDS WITH VISUAL STIMULI

MATERIALS: A Pictures.

TASK INSTRUCTIONS: Arrange the stimulus items in two rows of five.

CLINICIAN INSTRUCTIONS: "I'm going to have you do some things with each of these. Listen carefully and do just what I tell you to do."

SUGGESTED CRITERIA: 90 percent accuracy without the need of repetition of the task instructions or significant delays in responding.

1. Touch the brush with the spoon.
2. Give me the watch or the phone.
3. Touch the spoon, the cup, and the brush.
4. Pick up the money and the watch, then smile.
5. Put the car or the book under the watch.
6. When I shrug my shoulders, hand me the cup and the spoon.
7. Pick up the brush instead of the car.
8. Put the cup and the spoon in the corner.
9. Turn over the cup, and put the spoon on top of it.
10. Put the watch under the cup, and give me the money.
11. When I pick up the car, you put the spoon in the corner.
12. Do not pick up the book unless you have read one.
13. Put the phone and the watch on the bed.
14. Touch the one you read, and give me the one you drink from.
15. Instead of picking up the book, touch the money.
16. Put the chair on the one you tell time with.
17. Do not pick up either the brush or the phone.
18. Put the one you sit on next to the one you spend.
19. Put the book on the chair and the phone in the corner.
20. Put the cup under the book, and point to the car.

FOLLOWING MULTIUNIT COMMANDS WITH VISUAL STIMULI

MATERIALS:	B Pictures.
TASK INSTRUCTIONS:	Arrange the stimulus items in two rows of five.
CLINICIAN INSTRUCTIONS:	"I'm going to have you do some things with each of these. Listen carefully and do just what I tell you to do."
SUGGESTED CRITERIA:	90 percent accuracy without the need of repetition of the task instructions or significant delays in responding.

1. Touch the one you ring, but pick up the one you cut wood with.
2. Touch the umbrella and the kite, and give me the radio.
3. Instead of touching the tent, pick up the pipe and give it to me.
4. Put the refrigerator on the saddle, and point to the flashlight.
5. Put the bell with the radio when I touch the one you use in the rain.
6. Together with the kite and the saw, touch the tent.
7. Put the pipe with the refrigerator, and turn over the saddle.
8. Pick up the flashlight while you give me the one you ring.
9. Put the radio on the umbrella and the kite on the saddle.
10. Give me the pipe and the saw, then turn over the one you sleep in.
11. Turn the refrigerator upside down, and put the saddle on the flashlight.
12. Touch the bell and the umbrella, and turn over the radio and the kite.
13. Pick up the saw and the tent together with the one you listen to.
14. Point to the saddle and flashlight and turn over the kite and the bell.
15. Put the radio and the umbrella with the saw, and give me the tent.

16. Touch the pipe with the refrigerator, and lift the bell and flashlight.
17. Turn over the saddle and the radio, and give me the one you tell time with.
18. Put the kite, tent, and saw in a pile, then point to the bell.
19. Give me the one you put food in, then point to the pipe and the saddle.
20. Put the one you fly in the sky next to the one you put on a horse.

FOLLOWING MULTIUNIT COMMANDS WITH VISUAL STIMULI

MATERIALS:	C Pictures.
TASK INSTRUCTIONS:	Arrange the stimulus items in two rows of five.
CLINICIAN INSTRUCTIONS:	"I'm going to have you do some things with each of these. Listen carefully and do just what I tell you to do." *Note:* After delivering the stimuli, the clinician should randomly alternate the order of his/her gestures.
SUGGESTED CRITERIA:	90 percent accuracy without the need of repetition of the task instructions or significant delays in responding.

1. When I look at the floor, touch the lawn mower; when I look at the ceiling, touch the scale.
2. When I nod my head once, touch the calendar; when I nod twice, touch the parachute.
3. When I raise my hand, touch the fire hydrant; when I wave it, touch the stapler.
4. When I smile, touch the battery; when I wink, touch the camera.
5. When I shrug, touch the envelope; when I scratch my head, touch the helicopter.
6. When I close one eye, turn over the parachute; when I close both eyes, turn over the lawn mower.
7. When I close my fist, pick up the scale; when I open it, pick up the fire hydrant.
8. When I touch my nose, give me the calendar; when I touch my ear, give me the stapler.
9. When I say "hello," touch the camera; when I say "goodbye," touch the battery.
10. When I point to you, turn over the envelope; when I point to myself, turn over the helicopter.
11. When I nod my head, turn over the scale; when I wink, pick up the parachute.

12. When I touch my chin, touch the camera; when I shrug, give me the lawn mower.
13. When I make a fist, point to the stapler; when I raise my hand, pick up the fire hydrant.
14. When I put up one finger, touch the battery; when I put up two, turn over the envelope.
15. When I say "yes," touch the helicopter; when I say "no," pick up the scale.
16. When I look at my watch, give me the parachute; when I look at the wall, pick up the stapler.
17. When I tap once, point to the lawn mower; when I tap twice, turn over the camera.
18. When I smile, touch the calendar; when I frown, pick up the envelope.
19. When I touch my shoulder, touch the scale; when I touch my knee, turn over the battery.
20. When I cover my nose, give me the stapler; when I cover my mouth, touch the fire hydrant.

ANSWERING MULTIUNIT YES-NO QUESTIONS

MATERIALS:	None.
TASK INSTRUCTIONS:	Ask the patient questions without the presence of the visual stimuli.
CLINICIAN INSTRUCTIONS:	"I'm going to ask you some questions, and I want you to answer/indicate yes or no."
SUGGESTED CRITERIA:	90 percent accuracy without the need of repetition of the task instructions or significant delays in responding.

1. Do people wear coats to keep cold?
2. Do people eat food when they are hungry?
3. Can you run as fast as a bird can fly?
4. Can you breathe with your head under water?
5. Do toads and frogs have feathers?
6. Can a boy seven years old have a mustache?
7. Can you touch your left elbow with your left hand?
8. Would a stream you can wade across be good for boating?
9. Do cars travel as fast as speeding trains?
10. Do wingless birds fly over trees?
11. Do mice run away when they are scared?
12. Do people seek shelter during a rain storm?
13. Does a baby eat as much as an adult?
14. Do turtles wear shells on their backs?
15. Will tools rust if they are left out in the rain?
16. Do watches tell the correct time if they are broken?
17. Do you serve food on soiled dishes?
18. Can a hot plate melt butter?
19. Are naughty children pleasant company?
20. Do barbers cut hair with dull shears?

ANSWERING MULTIUNIT YES-NO QUESTIONS

MATERIALS: None.

TASK INSTRUCTIONS: Ask the patient questions
                           without the presence of the
                           visual stimuli.

CLINICIAN INSTRUCTIONS: "I'm going to ask you some
                           questions, and I want you to
                           answer/indicate yes or no."

SUGGESTED CRITERIA: 90 percent accuracy without the
                           need of repetition of the task
                           instructions or significant delays
                           in responding.

1. Do people eat food when they are hungry?
2. Can you write a message with an empty pen?
3. Do engineless cars go as fast as bicycles?
4. Is Nancy, Fred's cousin, a girl?
5. Do you season milk with salt before drinking it?
6. Can you get a chair over here by telling it to come?
7. Will a wooden block bounce as high as a ball?
8. Can you scratch the back of your left hand with a finger of that hand?
9. Are airplanes the only things that fly?
10. Are elephants and hippos big animals?
11. Can you see both the moon and the sun at night?
12. Do we wear belts to keep our socks up?
13. Do we put sugar in some of our food to make it taste better?
14. Do watches and clocks tell time?
15. Do we read newspapers, magazines, and pens?
16. Are boots, slippers, and shoes things you wear on your feet?
17. Do you need tools to change a tire?
18. Do you have ten fingers on your feet?
19. Will a glass break as easily as a plastic plate?
20. Are oranges, coal, and apples tasty fruit?

ANSWERING MULTI UNIT YES-NO QUESTIONS

MATERIALS:	None.
TASK INSTRUCTIONS:	Ask the patient questions without the presence of the visual stimuli.
CLINICIAN INSTRUCTIONS:	"I'm going to ask you some questions, and I want you to answer/indicate yes or no."
SUGGESTED CRITERIA:	90 percent accuracy without the need of repetition of the task instructions or significant delays in responding.

1. Would you put hot soup in an ice box to keep it warm?
2. Are snow, ice, and books all cold?
3. Are horses the only animals we ride on?
4. Are there seven days in a week and nine months in a year?
5. Will a retracted umbrella protect you from the rain?
6. Does a dog have paws and a tail?
7. Can a disabled duck swim and fly?
8. Is a bath towel useful when it is not dry?
9. Are clothes hangers always made of wood?
10. Can a lion hurt you when he is not in a cage?
11. Does the paperboy deliver mail every morning?
12. Does a dog wag his tail all of the time?
13. Do you sharpen a pencil so that you can erase better?
14. Will rain get you wet if you have not sought shelter?
15. Are cheese, coffee, and eggs all dairy products?
16. Do children usually have grey hair?
17. Are quarters, dimes, and nickels all money?
18. Do all boats need motors?
19. Do you need to use water with soap in order to get lather?
20. Will ice cubes melt while stored in a freezer?

ANSWERING MULTIUNIT YES-NO QUESTIONS

MATERIALS:	None.
TASK INSTRUCTIONS:	Ask the patient questions without the presence of the visual stimuli.
CLINICIAN INSTRUCTIONS:	"I'm going to ask you some questions, and I want you to answer/indicate yes or no."
SUGGESTED CRITERIA:	90 percent accuracy without the need of repetition of the task instructions or significant delays in responding.

1. Will meat spoil if not stored in a refrigerator?
2. Do women wear makeup to improve their appearance?
3. Do we use potholders to prevent our arms from burning?
4. Are tables, chairs, and trees all furniture?
5. Are toy trains operated by engineers?
6. Do you put paper plates in a dishwasher?
7. Are cars, trains, and airplanes all modes of transportation?
8. Will you burn your hands if you put them on a rock?
9. Do tailors use needles and thread to mend their clothes?
10. Is Christmas the same day in December each year?
11. Do children go trick or treating on Thanksgiving?
12. Are fire and ice the same temperature?
13. Do a flashlight and a lamp provide equal light?
14. Can you buy the same amount of food with a dime as with fifty cents?
15. Are watches and sundials both time pieces?
16. Do all criminals receive justice?
17. Are two pounds of flour as heavy as one?
18. Does a long pole help a tightrope walker to keep in balance?
19. Do you use your chest when you breathe in?
20. Are temperatures of freezing and boiling in opposition?

ANSWERING MULTIUNIT YES-NO QUESTIONS

MATERIALS:	None.
TASK INSTRUCTIONS:	Ask the patient questions without the presence of the visual stimuli.
CLINICIAN INSTRUCTIONS:	"I'm going to ask you some questions, and I want you to answer/indicate yes or no."
SUGGESTED CRITERIA:	90 percent accuracy without the need of repetition of the task instructions or significant delays in responding.

1. Can you wear a waterproof watch while swimming?
2. Do you write with a pencil if you wish to keep something permanent?
3. Do you drink water to increase your appetite?
4. Do you eat food to subdue your thirst?
5. Are knives, forks, and books all eating utensils?
6. Are lions and tigers dangerous animals?
7. Can you put two pieces of paper together with staples or glue?
8. Do you put food in the ice chest to keep it frozen?
9. Can you go to the grocery store to buy a chain saw?
10. Can you buy toothpaste at a stationery store?
11. Are sixty seconds equal to one hour?
12. Can a pin perforate and destroy an inflated balloon?
13. Will a plant's growth be retarded if it is not watered?
14. Would falling on a beach hurt as much as falling on concrete?
15. Do dentists recommend brushing your teeth three times an hour?
16. Will you see the sky and the ground by gazing upward?
17. Does a warm drink cool you down on a hot summer's day?
18. Would you go to a veterinarian for treatment of a cold?
19. Do you need both of your hands to comb your hair?
20. Does a truck driver rest while he is driving at night?

FOLLOWING MULTIUNIT COMMANDS—
TEMPORAL RELATIONS

MATERIALS: A Pictures.

TASK INSTRUCTIONS: Arrange the stimulus items in
two rows of five.

CLINICIAN INSTRUCTIONS: "I'm going to have you do some
things with each of these. Listen
carefully and do just what I tell
you to do."

SUGGESTED CRITERIA: 90 percent accuracy without the
need of repetition of the task
instructions or significant delays
in responding.

1. After I nod my head, pick up the spoon.
2. Touch the cup after I raise my hand.
3. Before I look at the ceiling, pick up the phone.
4. After I point to you, turn over the watch.
5. Give me the bed after I wink.
6. After I shrug my shoulders, pick up the brush.
7. Turn over the book before I nod my head.
8. Before I smile, touch the money.
9. Point to the chair after I say "Now".
10. After you point to the spoon, point to me.
11. After I touch the car, you touch it.
12. Point to the brush before I do.
13. Touch the chair after I do.
14. Before I touch the watch, you touch it.
15. After you raise your hand, touch the cup.
16. Touch the phone before I do.
17. After I pick up the money, you pick it up.
18. Smile before you give me the spoon.
19. After you turn over the book, wink.
20. Nod your head after you give me the watch.

FOLLOWING MULTIUNIT COMMANDS—
TEMPORAL RELATIONS

MATERIALS:	B Pictures.
TASK INSTRUCTIONS:	Arrange the stimulus items in two rows of five.
CLINICIAN INSTRUCTIONS:	"I'm going to have you do some things with each of these. Listen carefully and do just what I tell you to do."
SUGGESTED CRITERIA:	90 percent accuracy without the need of repetition of the task instructions or significant delays in responding.

1. After you touch the flashlight, touch the bell.
2. Pick up the radio after you touch the umbrella.
3. Before you give me the tent, turn over the refrigerator.
4. Pick up the saddle before you touch the saw.
5. After touching the pipe, give me the kite.
6. Before turning over the bell, pick up the umbrella.
7. Touch the radio after you give me the tent.
8. After picking up the saddle, point to the refrigerator.
9. Before turning over the saw, give me the saw.
10. Turn over the pipe after picking up the bell.
11. After turning over the umbrella, pick up the radio.
12. Before touching the tent, give me the saddle.
13. Pick up the pipe after you touch the refrigerator.
14. Point to the radio before you turn over the bell.
15. Give me the kite after you touch the saw.
16. Touch the flashlight after you touch the saddle.
17. Before you point to the tent, touch the refrigerator.
18. After you pick up the radio, point to the saw.
19. Turn over the umbrella before you give me the flashlight.
20. Give me the tent after you touch the pipe.

FOLLOWING MULTIUNIT COMMANDS—
TEMPORAL RELATIONS

MATERIALS:	C Pictures.
TASK INSTRUCTIONS:	Arrange the stimulus items in two rows of five. The clinician can substitute "before" and "after" in each stimulus.
CLINICIAN INSTRUCTIONS:	"I'm going to have you do some things with certain objects. Listen carefully and do just what I tell you to do."
SUGGESTED CRITERIA:	90 percent accuracy without the need of repetition of the task instructions or significant delays in responding.

1. Give me the helicopter after you touch the calendar and the scale.
2. Before you pick up the stapler and the battery, touch the camera.
3. After you give me the parachute, turn over the envelope and the helicopter.
4. Touch the lawn mower and scale after you pick up the fire hydrant.
5. Point to the stapler before you turn over the calendar and the battery.
6. Before you touch the camera and the parachute, give me the envelope.
7. After you turn over the scale and the fire hydrant, pick up the helicopter.
8. Give me the battery before you touch the lawn mower and the stapler.
9. Turn over the camera and the calendar before you give me the parachute.
10. Touch the envelope after you point to the helicopter and the fire hydrant.
11. Before you turn over the scale and the stapler, touch the battery and the camera.

12. After you give me the lawn mower and the calendar, touch the parachute.
13. Pick up the envelope before you touch the helicopter and the scale.
14. Point to the fire hydrant and the stapler before you give me the battery.
15. Turn over the lawn mower and the camera after you touch the calendar.
16. After you give me the parachute, pick up the envelope and helicopter.
17. Before you touch the stapler and the battery, touch the lawn mower.
18. After you turn over the camera, touch the parachute and the envelope.
19. Give me the stapler after you point to the battery and the calendar.
20. Touch the lawn mower and the fire hydrant before you give me the helicopter.

FOLLOWING MULTIUNIT COMMANDS—*SPATIAL RELATIONS*

MATERIALS:	A Pictures.
TASK INSTRUCTIONS:	Arrange the stimulus items in two rows of five.
CLINICIAN INSTRUCTIONS:	"I'm going to have you do some things with each of these. Listen carefully and do just what I tell you to do."
SUGGESTED CRITERIA:	90 percent accuracy without the need of repetition of the task instructions or significant delays in responding.

1. Put the spoon under the book.
2. Put the brush on the chair.
3. Put the phone behind the bed.
4. Put the car next to the cup.
5. Put the money in front of the watch.
6. Put the book on the chair.
7. Put the brush under the spoon.
8. Put the phone next to the car.
9. Put the cup behind the bed.
10. Put the watch in front of the chair.
11. Put the book on the money.
12. Put the phone under the brush.
13. Put the car next to the spoon.
14. Put the cup in front of the watch.
15. Put the chair behind the bed.
16. Put the phone under the book.
17. Put the money on the brush.
18. Put the car next to the cup.
19. Put the watch on the spoon.
20. Put the chair in front of the phone.

FOLLOWING MULTIUNIT COMMANDS—*SPATIAL RELATIONS*

MATERIALS:	B Pictures.
TASK INSTRUCTIONS:	Arrange stimulus materials in two rows of five. Place the pictures in the following order. First row: Bell, radio, umbrella, kite, saw. Second row: Tent, pipe, refrigerator, saddle, flashlight.
CLINICIAN INSTRUCTIONS:	"I'm going to have you do some things with certain objects. Listen carefully and do just what I tell you to do."
SUGGESTED CRITERIA:	90 percent accuracy without the need of repetition of the task instructions or significant delays in responding.

1. Put the bell to the left of the radio.
2. Put the umbrella to the right of the kite.
3. Put the saw between the tent and the pipe.
4. Put the saddle to the left of the refrigerator.
5. Put the bell between the umbrella and the kite.
6. Put the saw to the right of the pipe.
7. Put the saddle to the left of the bell.
8. Put the refrigerator between the radio and the umbrella.
9. Put the saw between the tent and the pipe.
10. Put the refrigerator under the kite.
11. Put the flashlight to the right of the radio.
12. Put the pipe between the refrigerator and the saddle.
13. Put the kite on the saw.
14. Put the flashlight to the right of the bell.
15. Put the tent behind the kite.
16. Put the refrigerator between the flashlight and the saddle.
17. Put the bell under the radio.
18. Put the flashlight to the left of the kite.
19. Put the umbrella between the pipe and the refrigerator.
20. Put the saw between the flashlight and the saddle.

FOLLOWING MULTIUNIT COMMANDS—*SPATIAL RELATIONS*

MATERIALS:	C Pictures.
TASK INSTRUCTIONS:	Arrange the stimulus items in two rows of five.
CLINICIAN INSTRUCTIONS:	"I'm going to have you do some things with each of these. Listen carefully and do just what I tell you to do."
SUGGESTED CRITERIA:	90 percent accuracy without the need of repetition of the task instructions or significant delays in responding.

1. Put the calendar under the scale and the helicopter behind it.
2. Put the parachute on the stapler and the camera under it.
3. Put the lawn mower next to the fire hydrant and the envelope behind it.
4. Put the stapler in front of the scale and the helicopter under it.
5. Put the battery on the envelope and the helicopter next to it.
6. Put the calendar behind the parachute and the camera to the right of it.
7. Put the lawn mower under the envelope and the fire hydrant to the left of it.
8. Put the stapler on the calendar and the battery in front of it.
9. Put the helicopter to the right of the camera and the scale to the left of it.
10. Put the envelope under the fire hydrant and the battery behind it.
11. Put the parachute next to the calendar and the lawn mower under it.
12. Put the scale to the left of the stapler and the camera in front of it.
13. Put the helicopter on the envelope and the battery to the right of it.
14. Put the fire hydrant behind the parachute and the calendar next to it.

15. Put the lawn mower to the right of the camera and the scale to the left of it.
16. Put the stapler on the envelope and the helicopter next to it.
17. Put the calendar in front of the parachute and the fire hydrant under it.
18. Put the scale next to the battery and the camera behind it.
19. Put the envelope under the helicopter and the lawn mower on top of it.
20. Put the fire hydrant in front of the parachute and the stapler next to it.

FOLLOWING IF-THEN COMMANDS WITH VISUAL STIMULI

MATERIALS:	A Pictures.
TASK INSTRUCTIONS:	Arrange the stimulus items in two rows of five.
CLINICIAN INSTRUCTIONS:	"I'm going to have you do some things with each of these. Listen carefully and do just what I tell you to do."
SUGGESTED CRITERIA:	90 percent accuracy without the need of repetition of the task instructions or significant delays in responding.

1. If there is something to eat with, touch it; if not, shake your head.
2. If there is something to cut with, pick it up; if not, point to the ceiling.
3. If there is something to shave with, point to it; if not, shrug your shoulders.
4. If there is something to read, turn it over; if not, raise your hand.
5. If there is something to swim in, touch it; if not, shake your head.
6. If there is something to chew on, point to it; if not, wink.
7. If there is something to sleep on, turn it over; if not, touch the cup.
8. If there is something that has wheels, turn it over; if not, touch the bed.
9. If there is something to drink from, pick it up; if not, touch the money.
10. If there is something to write with, point to it; if not, touch the brush.
11. If there is something to bake, touch it; if not, turn over the car.
12. If there is something to fix hair with, pick it up; if not, give me the watch.
13. If there is something to tell time with, give it to me; if not, turn over the bed.

14. If there is something to sit on, touch it; if not, touch the thing you drive.
15. If there is something to blow your nose with, touch it; if not, give me the thing that has pages.
16. If there is something that has bristles on it, turn it over; if not, touch the thing that ticks.
17. If there is something to call people on, pick it up; if not, touch the thing that has four legs.
18. If there is something to erase with, turn it over; if not, give me the thing you wear on your wrist.
19. If there is something you spend, touch it; if not, touch the thing you read.
20. If there is something to wear on your feet, give it to me; if not, turn over the thing that rings.

FOLLOWING IF-THEN BODY PART COMMANDS

MATERIALS:	None.
TASK INSTRUCTIONS:	Arrange the stimulus items in two rows of five.
CLINICIAN INSTRUCTIONS:	"I'm going to have you do some things with certain parts of your body. listen carefully and dojust what I tell you to do."
SUGGESTED CRITERIA:	90 percent accuracy without the need of repetition of the task instructions or significant delays in responding.

1. If you have a hat on, raise your hand; if not, shake your head.
2. If over and under mean the same thing, look at the ceiling; if not, point to me.
3. If there are seven days in a week, nod your head; if not, touch your knee.
4. If corn is grown in the United States, shrug your shoulders; if not, lift your foot.
5. If your name is John, hold up two fingers; if not, put up four.
6. If I am wearing my coat, nod your head; if not, look around for it.
7. If I have red hair look at it; if not, touch your head.
8. If you have ever lived in Alaska, raise your hand; if not, wink at me.
9. If you are wearing a necklace, point to it; if not, shake your head.
10. If there is a clock in this room, point to it; if not, point to your wrist.
11. If I have pants on, smile at me; if not, shake your head.
12. If both ice and snow are cold, tug at your ear; if not, close your eyes.
13. If there are twelve months in a year, raise your hand; if not, point to me.
14. If I am the only person you've seen today, look at the ceiling; if not, look at the floor.

15. If only women grow mustaches, point to your lips; if not, point to your neck.
16. If I am wearing a watch, point to it; if not, look at the ceiling.
17. If a giraffe has a short neck, point to your neck; if not, point to mine.
18. If lemons and grapefruits are sour, purse your lips; if not, smile at me.
19. If there is a telephone in here, point to it; if not, point to your ear.
20. If broken watches tell time, nod your head; if not, point to your wrist.

FOLLOWING IF-THEN BODY PART COMMANDS

MATERIALS: None.

TASK INSTRUCTIONS: None.

CLINICIAN INSTRUCTIONS: "I'm going to have you do some things with certain parts of your body. Listen carefully and do just what I tell you to do."

SUGGESTED CRITERIA: 90 percent accuracy without the need of repetition of the task instructions or significant delays in responding.

1. If four is less than three, scratch your head; if not, scratch your knee.
2. If you are a man or a woman, nod your head; if not, smile.
3. If an elephant is larger than a horse, point to the floor; if not, raise your hand.
4. If you are older than I am, smile; if not, shake your head.
5. If a chicken has more legs than a pig, put up four fingers; if not, put up two.
6. If twelve is more than ten, raise your hand; if not, clench your fist.
7. If you are the only person in this room, put up one finger; if not, put up two.
8. If winter comes after fall, point to me; if not, touch your nose.
9. If the floor is above you, point to it; if not, shake your head.
10. If a closet is bigger than a bedroom, smile; if not, point to the door.
11. If your thumb is next to your index finger, put up your thumb; if not, put up your index finger.
12. If a plant is smaller than a tree, point to me; if not, touch your knee.
13. If you have more teeth than fingernails, nod your head; if not, touch your forehead.
14. If Christmas comes just before Thanksgiving, point to the ceiling; if not, smile.
15. If a snake is longer than a worm, wiggle your finger; if not, close your eyes.

16. If five is more than seven, raise your hand; if not, shrug your shoulders.
17. If bushes are shorter than trees, nod your head; if not, smile.
18. If watches are larger than clocks, look at the wall; if not, look at your wrist.
19. If it is night now, point to the ceiling; if not, point to the floor.
20. If you have shorter hair than I do, touch your hair; if not, point to me.

ANSWERING MULTIUNIT YES-NO
QUESTIONS—*COMPARATIVES*

MATERIALS:	None.
TASK INSTRUCTIONS:	None.
CLINICIAN INSTRUCTIONS:	"I'm going to ask you some questions, and I want you to answer/indicate yes or no."
SUGGESTED CRITERIA:	90 percent accuracy without the need of repetition of the task instructions or significant delays in responding.

1. Is a briefcase bigger than a suitcase?
2. Is a nail bigger than a pin?
3. Is a stone softer than an orange?
4. Are your teeth harder than your fingernails?
5. Is a mouse smaller than a cat?
6. Are your ears closer together than your eyes?
7. Is an egg heavier than a balloon?
8. Is your thumb shorter than your little toe?
9. Is a worm longer than a snake?
10. Does an apple have more juice than an orange?
11. Can a dog run faster than a turtle?
12. Does a butterfly have larger wings than a bee?
13. Are your ears larger than a rabbit's ears?
14. Does a helicopter fly faster than a jet plane?
15. Is a clock bigger than a watch?
16. Is a kitten less dangerous than a lion?
17. Does a table have more legs than you do?
18. Is a streetlight farther away than the moon?
19. Can you carry more things in one hand than in two?
20. Are there more pages in a thick book than in a thin book?

ANSWERING MULTIUNIT YES-NO
QUESTIONS—*COMPARATIVES*

MATERIALS: None.

TASK INSTRUCTIONS: None.

CLINICIAN INSTRUCTIONS: "I'm going to ask you some questions, and I want you to answer/indicate yes or no."

SUGGESTED CRITERIA: 90 percent accuracy without the need of repetition of the task instructions or significant delays in responding.

1. Does it take longer to put on a hat than to tie shoes?
2. Will wet paper burn faster than dry paper?
3. Would a pony be easier to ride than a rooster?
4. Do boots cover more of your legs than shoes do?
5. Do you have more inches around your neck than around your waist?
6. Would it take longer to fly to Chicago than to walk there?
7. Do little dogs eat more than big dogs?
8. Are there less stores in a city than in a town?
9. Does a tree have more leaves on it than a bush?
10. Is a dry log heavier than a wet log?
11. Are newspaper pages larger than pages in a book?
12. Will a glass break less easily than a plastic cup?
13. Is ink easier to erase than a pencil?
14. Will a carpet cover more of a floor than a door mat?
15. Will a handkerchief rip more easily than a paper tissue?
16. Will a sharpened knife cut more easily than a dull knife?
17. Does a swimming pool hold less water than a bathtub?
18. Can you throw a baseball farther than a balloon?
19. Do eyeglasses magnify more than binoculars?
20. Does a garbage can hold less than a wastebasket?

ANSWERING MULTIUNIT YES-NO QUESTIONS—*TEMPORAL RELATIONS*

MATERIALS: None.

TASK INSTRUCTIONS: Ask the patient questions. Clinician can substitute "before" and "after" in each stimulus.

CLINICIAN INSTRUCTIONS: "I'm going to ask you some questions, and I want you to answer/indicate yes or no."

SUGGESTED CRITERIA: 90 percent accuracy without the need of repetition of the task instructions or significant delays in responding.

1. Do people eat dessert before dinner?
2. Are streets wet after a rainstorm?
3. Do you light a fire after you have struck the match?
4. Do you put ice cubes in your drink after you have finished the drink?
5. Do you put icing on a cake before the cake is made?
6. Does Christmas come after Thanksgiving?
7. Does five come after four?
8. Do you put a stamp on a letter after you have mailed it?
9. Do you get out of the plane before it has landed?
10. Does ice melt after it comes out of the freezer?
11. Do people put on their pajamas after they fall asleep?
12. Do you dry yourself after you come out of the shower?
13. Do you start the car before you get in it?
14. Do you put on your raincoat before you go into the rainstorm?
15. Do you put your socks on before you put your shoes on?
16. Do you turn a light on in a room after you have left it?
17. Do people eat breakfast before they wake up in the morning?
18. Does a laundress dry clothes after she has washed them?
19. Does February come after January?
20. Do you watch T.V. after you fall asleep?

ANSWERING MULTIUNIT YES-NO QUESTIONS—*TEMPORAL RELATIONS*

MATERIALS:	None.
TASK INSTRUCTIONS:	Ask the patient questions. Clinician can substitute "before" and "after" in each stimulus.
CLINICIAN INSTRUCTIONS:	"I'm going to ask you some questions, and I want you to answer/indicate yes or no."
SUGGESTED CRITERIA:	90 percent accuracy without the need of repetition of the task instructions or significant delays in responding.

1. Do you drink coffee before it is poured into the cup?
2. Do you erase a mistake after you have made it?
3. Do you put on your sweater after you have put on your shirt?
4. Do you empty the wastebasket after it is filled?
5. Do you put salt on your egg before you fry it?
6. Can you listen to the radio after you have turned it off?
7. Do you mend a shirt before it rips?
8. Were you born before I was?
9. Do you wind a clock after it has stopped ticking?
10. Does a child go to the third grade before he goes to the first grade?
11. Does breakfast come before lunch?
12. Was your mother born before you were?
13. Do you answer a phone before it starts ringing?
14. Do carpenters put on the roof of a house before they have laid the foundation?
15. Does the T.V. picture come on after you have turned it on?
16. Do you put on your swimsuit after you have gone swimming?
17. Do you open a door after someone has knocked?
18. Does a bar of soap produce lather after you add water?
19. Will a fire warm a room before you have lit it?
20. Do you seal an envelope before you put a letter in it?

ANSWERING MULTIUNIT YES-NO QUESTIONS—*SPATIAL RELATIONS*

MATERIALS:	None.
TASK INSTRUCTIONS:	None.
CLINICIAN INSTRUCTIONS:	"I'm going to ask you some questions, and I want you to answer/indicate yes or no."
SUGGESTED CRITERIA:	90 percent accuracy without the need of repetition of the task instructions or significant delays in responding.

1. Is your neck above your chin?
2. Do we read from right to left?
3. Is your heart above your knees?
4. Is New York east of California?
5. Is your nose above your mouth?
6. Is Canada south of the United States?
7. Is the floor above our heads?
8. Is there a chair over you?
9. Do you carry an umbrella over your head?
10. Are wheels under a car?
11. Do you pack clothes outside your suitcase?
12. Is there a table in front of you?
13. Do you wear a shirt over your sweater?
14. Do you put jelly between two pieces of bread to make a sandwich?
15. Do you wear a coat over your clothes?
16. Are your teeth inside your mouth?
17. Is your hair on top of your head?
18. Do you wear your shoes over your socks?
19. Do you wear a belt inside your waist?
20. Is your head between your ears?

ANSWERING MULTIUNIT YES-NO QUESTIONS—*SPATIAL RELATIONS*

MATERIALS: None.

TASK INSTRUCTIONS: None.

CLINICIAN INSTRUCTIONS: "I'm going to ask you some questions, and I want you to answer/indicate yes or no."

SUGGESTED CRITERIA: 90 percent accuracy without the need of repetition of the task instructions or significant delays in responding.

1. Is the ceiling under our feet?
2. Are pages between the cover of a book?
3. Does a sailboat travel under water?
4. Are the roots of a plant under the ground?
5. Is the engine of a train behind the caboose?
6. Do you wear a ring between your fingers?
7. Are your feet below your ankles?
8. Do you wear a collar between your chin and your shoulders?
9. Do women put their purses in their wallets?
10. Is the number four between three and five?
11. Do you put a stamp on the left side of an envelope?
12. Is your wrist between your hand and your arm?
13. Is your chair between you and the floor?
14. Is your thumb between your little finger and your index finger?
15. Is the T.V. channel changer behind the T.V. set?
16. Is a sock worn between your boot and your shoe?
17. Is your chin between your neck and shoulders?
18. Does the driver of a car sit on the right-hand side of the car?
19. Is New York west of the Atlantic Ocean?
20. Is Mexico north of the United States?

PARAGRAPH COMPREHENSION

MY GRANDMOTHER

MATERIALS:	None.
TASK INSTRUCTIONS:	Read the paragraph to the patient at a moderate rate.
CLINICIAN INSTRUCTIONS:	"I'm going to read you a short paragraph. Listen carefully because I will ask you questions about the story when I have finished."
SUGGESTED CRITERIA:	90 percent accuracy without the need of repetition of the task instructions or significant delays in responding.

My grandmother is 95 years old. She lives in New York in a large, old house with a maid and a cook to care for her. She is deaf but reads lips well.

1. Is this about an old man?
2. Does she live in New York?
3. Does she live in a large, old house?
4. Do her children take care of her there?
5. Is she blind?

THE OLDEST MAN

MATERIALS:	None.
TASK INSTRUCTIONS:	Read the paragraph to the patient at a moderate rate.
CLINICIAN INSTRUCTIONS:	"I'm going to read you a short paragraph. Listen carefully because I will ask you questions about the story when I have finished."
SUGGESTED CRITERIA:	90 percent accuracy without the need of repetition of the task instructions or significant delays in responding.

Charlie Smith is the oldest person in the world. He is 136 years old and lives in a nursing home. At the age of 12, he was brought to the United States as a slave, but the Civil War freed him. He was married three times and worked until he was 113.

1. Was Charlie Smith born in the United States?
2. Is he over 130 years old?
3. Does he live by himself?
4. Was he ever married?
5. Did he stop working when he was 100?

CAULIFLOWER

MATERIALS:	None.
TASK INSTRUCTIONS:	Read the paragraph to the patient at a moderate rate.
CLINICIAN INSTRUCTIONS:	"I'm going to read you a short paragraph. Listen carefully because I will ask you questions about the story when I have finished."
SUGGESTED CRITERIA:	90 percent accuracy without the need of repetition of the task instructions or significant delays in responding.

Cooking a cauliflower calls for great care. It must not be allowed to get even slightly mushy. The simplest way to avoid this is to cook it in a pan just large enough to hold the head comfortably. Pour in one inch of water and add salt. Cover it with a lid and cook at high heat for 15 minutes.

1. Is this paragraph about broccoli?
2. Does it matter how long you cook it?
3. Do they suggest using a frying pan?
4. Do they suggest using many herbs?
5. Should you cover the pan while cooking?

MCDONALD'S HAMBURGERS

MATERIALS: None.

TASK INSTRUCTIONS: Read the paragraph to the
                          patient at a moderate rate.

CLINICIAN INSTRUCTIONS: "I'm going to read you a short
                          paragraph. Listen carefully
                          because I will ask you questions
                          about the story when I have
                          finished."

SUGGESTED CRITERIA: 90 percent accuracy without the
                          need of repetition of the task
                          instructions or significant delays
                          in responding.

   The first McDonald's hamburger stand came into existence in 1954 in
San Bernadino, California. It was owned by two brothers, Maurice and
Richard McDonald. A salesman named Ray Kroc bought out the
McDonald brothers in 1960 and made the hamburgers famous. By 1978,
27 billion McDonald hamburgers had been sold.

1. Was this paragraph about how to make hamburgers?
2. Did the first stand come into existence in 1960?
3. Was it in San Bernadino?
4. Does the McDonald family still own the stands?
5. Had more than 20 billion hamburgers been sold by 1978?

HORSERADISH

MATERIALS:	None.
TASK INSTRUCTIONS:	Read the paragraph to the patient at a moderate rate.
CLINICIAN INSTRUCTIONS:	"I'm going to read you a short paragraph. Listen carefully because I will ask you questions about the story when I have finished."
SUGGESTED CRITERIA:	90 percent accuracy without the need of repetition of the task instructions or significant delays in responding.

Horseradish, which has its origins in eastern Europe, has been grown for centuries. The leaves and stems of this plant contain poison, but the root is safe in the amounts used by horseradish eaters. This plant is no trouble to grow; in fact, you may experience difficulty stopping it from taking over your garden!

1. Is this paragraph about a plant?
2. Does it originate in Canada?
3. Is the root safe to eat?
4. Does it grow easily?
5. Has it been grown for less than a century?

HOWARD HUGHES

MATERIALS:	None.
TASK INSTRUCTIONS:	Read the paragraph to the patient at a moderate rate.
CLINICIAN INSTRUCTIONS:	"I'm going to read you a short paragraph. Listen carefully because I will ask you questions about the story when I have finished."
SUGGESTED CRITERIA:	90 percent accuracy without the need of repetition of the task instructions or significant delays in responding.

The famous billionaire Howard Hughes was born in 1905 in Houston, Texas. His father died when Howard was 18, leaving him with a large fortune. During the 1930s and 1940s, he invested in airplanes and motion pictures and began building his billion dollar empire. In 1952, however, he went into total seclusion. The last ten years of his life were spent in his Desert Inn Hotel in Las Vegas. He died in 1976.

1. Is this paragraph about a billionaire?
2. Was Howard Hughes poor when he was 18?
3. Did he make his fortune in oil?
4. Did he live in a hotel the last years of his life?
5. Did he die in 1960?

MONACO

MATERIALS:	None.
TASK INSTRUCTIONS:	Read the paragraph to the patient at a moderate rate.
CLINICIAN INSTRUCTIONS:	"I'm going to read you a short paragraph. Listen carefully because I will ask you questions about the story when I have finished."
SUGGESTED CRITERIA:	90 percent accuracy without the need of repetition of the task instructions or significant delays in responding.

Monaco is a country that lies a few miles west of Italy. It is ruled by Prince Ranier and Princess Grace. It is surrounded by France and the Mediterranean Sea. It is famous for the Monte Carlo Casino, which makes so much money that the people of Monaco do not pay taxes. Monaco must be careful, though. Because of a treaty made with Paris in 1918, the country will fall to France if a male does not inherit the throne.

1. Is this a paragraph about a country?
2. Is it located in Italy?
3. Do people pay taxes in Monaco?
4. Is it because of casino profits that no taxes are paid?
5. May a princess rule Monaco?

NANTUCKET

MATERIALS:	None.
TASK INSTRUCTIONS:	Read the paragraph to the patient at a moderate rate.
CLINICIAN INSTRUCTIONS:	"I'm going to read you a short paragraph. Listen carefully because I will ask you questions about the story when I have finished."
SUGGESTED CRITERIA:	90 percent accuracy without the need of repetition of the task instructions or significant delays in responding.

Nantucket is a small, quaint island 30 miles off the coast of Massachusetts. It was once a major center for the whaling industry. Nantucket men used to leave their homes and families for months to hunt whales. It was a dangerous business. On the roofs of Nantucket homes were enclosed porches called "widows' walks." The wives of the whalers used to climb to these porches to watch for their husbands' returning ships. Many ships, however, never returned; many wives were made widows. "Widows' walks" can still be seen on Nantucket, but whales are no longer hunted. The island's major industry now is tourism.

1. Is Nantucket an island?
2. Is it 30 miles off the coast of Maine?
3. Did the ships usually return after two or three weeks?
4. Are the "widows' walks" on the roofs of the houses?
5. Do Nantucketers still hunt whales?

THE DINNER

MATERIALS:	None.
TASK INSTRUCTIONS:	Read the paragraph to the patient at a moderate rate.
CLINICIAN INSTRUCTIONS:	"I'm going to read you a short paragraph. Listen carefully because I will ask you questions about the story when I have finished."
SUGGESTED CRITERIA:	90 percent accuracy without the need of repetition of the task instructions or significant delays in responding.

A young married man invited an old friend of his to come to his home for dinner. The young man's wife took her husband aside and told him she only had three pieces of chicken. Each person could only have one piece. He promised not to urge his friend to have more.

The husband forgot however, and during dinner, he urged his friend to have more. The wife looked distressed, and the friend declined. Her husband insisted, but the friend still refused. Later, she asked her husband, "How could you have urged him to have more chicken when we had none?" Her husband explained that he had forgotten. "Forgotten?" she said, "Why do you think I was kicking you?" "But you weren't kicking *me*," he said.

1. Were two people invited for dinner?
2. Did the wife ask her husband to send the friend home?
3. Did the wife serve chicken?
4. Was it possible for each person to have one piece of chicken?
5. Did the friend ask for more chicken?
6. Did the husband urge his friend to have more?
7. Was the wife pleased?
8. Did the wife kick the friend?
9. Did she kick him on purpose?
10. Do you think the wife was embarrassed when she realized what had happened?

MICHAEL MALLOY

MATERIALS: None.

TASK INSTRUCTIONS: Read the paragraph to the patient at a moderate rate.

CLINICIAN INSTRUCTIONS: "I'm going to read you a short paragraph. Listen carefully because I will ask you questions about the story when I have finished."

SUGGESTED CRITERIA: 90 percent accuracy without the need of repetition of the task instructions or significant delays in responding.

Michael Malloy was not an ordinary man; he was practically indestructible. Thirty attempts were made on his life; he survived them all.

In the early 1930s, Michael Malloy spent his days in a New York bar. Here, he came to the attention of a group of men desperately in need of money. Forming a partnership, these men befriended Malloy and took out a life insurance policy on him. Their plan was to murder him and cash in on the policy. To get the most out of the policy, they decided to make the death look like an accident.

At first, they simply gave the unsuspecting Malloy unlimited free drinks in the hope that he would drink himself to death. When this approach failed, they began adding antifreeze, wood alcohol, and turpentine to his drinks. Each night, Malloy would go home in a drunken stupor but return happily the next day, asking for more. Once, they put the drunk man outside in below zero temperature in an attempt to freeze him to death. Another time, they ran a car over him. No attempt succeeded in killing the incredible man. In desperation, the men finally murdered Malloy outright. They never collected the insurance money, however. All were either jailed or sentenced to death.

1. Was Michael Malloy a murderer?
2. Did he spend his days in a bar?
3. Did he get free drinks there?
4. Did the men wish to kill Malloy because they hated him?
5. Did they try to kill him with a gun?
6. Did he drink turpentine?
7. Did the drinks kill him?
8. Did they try to freeze him to death?
9. Is Michael Malloy still alive?
10. Were the men caught?

VERBAL EXPRESSION

SECTION TWO

VERBAL EXPRESSION

INTRODUCTION
SINGLE WORD RESPONSES
   Single Word Production—*Imitative*
   Single Word Sentence Completion—*Automatic*
   Single Word Sentence Completion—*Given Visual Stimuli*
   Single Word Sentence Completion—*Nouns*
   Single Word Sentence Completion—*Verbs*
   Single Word Response—*Response Provided in Stimulus*
   Single Word Response—*Recalling Nouns with Visual Cues*
   Single Word Response—*Recalling Common Nouns*
   Single Word Response—*Recalling Verbs*
   Single Word Response—*Recalling Places*
   Single Word Response—*Recalling Temporal Words*
   Single Word Response—*Recalling People*
   Single Word Response—*Recalling Difficult Nouns*
   Single Word Response—*Recall of Category Members*
   Single Word Response—*Recall of Categories*
TWO AND THREE WORD RESPONSES
   Two and Three Word Responses—*No Syntactic Restrictions*
   Phrase Production—*Response Provided in Stimulus*
   Phrase Production—*Stating Functions of Objects*
   Phrase Production—*Response to Questions*
   Phrase Production—*Sentence Completion*
SENTENCE FORMULATION
   Sentence Formulation—*Response to Questions*
   Sentence Formulation—*Given Noun Stimulus*
   Sentence Formulation—*Given Verb Stimulus*
   Sentence Formulation—*Given Adjective Stimulus*
   Sentence Formulation—*Given Functor Word Stimulus*
   Sentence Formulation—*Given Phrase Stimulus*
   Sentence Formulation—*Given Two Unrelated Words*

Sentence Formulation—*Question Production*
Sentence Formulation—*Given Introductory Sentence*
Sentence Formulation—*Unscrambling a Sentence*

COMPLEX SENTENCE FORMULATION
Description of Objects
Description of Animals and People
Description of Places
Answering "Why" Questions
Description of Likenesses and Differences
Explanation of Expressions
Definitions
Multiple Sentence and Phrase Formulation

PARAGRAPH FORMULATION
Paragraph Formulation
Retelling a Paragraph

INTRODUCTION

This section of the manual focuses treatment activities designed to improve skills of verbal expression. The treatment tasks designed and developed for this section include the following:

1. Tasks Requiring Single Word Responses.
    a. Imitative production of words
    b. Sentence completion
    c. Choice of response provided in stimulus
    d. Answering questions requiring single word responses
    e. Confrontation naming
    f. Recall of category members and categories
2. Tasks Requiring Two and Three Word Responses.
    a. Two and three word responses not bound by syntactic or morphemic rules
    b. Responses requiring syntactic constructions
3. Tasks Requiring Sentence Formulation Responses.
    a. Sentences describing function of objects
    b. Sentence formulation given single word, two words, or phrase stimuli or a scrambled set of words.
    c. Sentence formulation given introductory sentence or question.
4. Tasks Requiring Complex Verbal Responses.
    a. Object description
    b. Definition of words
    c. Interpretation of expressions
    d. Description of likenesses and differences
    e. Multiple phrase and sentence formulation
5. Tasks Requiring Paragraph Formulation.

The treatment tasks were selected and developed to improve verbal expressive skills of word recall, verbal sequencing, grammar, syntax, morphology, semantics, sentence formulation, and expression of abstract reasoning. The treatment activities are presented in a task hierarchy introducing those tasks requiring single unit responses and progressing to those tasks requiring complex verbal responses.

The variables that were considered in establishing the task hierarchy included the following:

1. *Length of response.* Two factors were considered. First, the total number of words required in the response, including small functor words. Second, the number of substantive units in the response.
2. *Automaticity of response.* Facilitating stimuli that trigger verbal responses were placed earlier in the task hierarchy. "Aphasic patients,

103

while unable to produce a given language response when they intend to do so, can sometimes produce it automatically in response to facilitating stimuli; that is, stimuli that triggers deeply rooted verbal habits."[1]

3. *Syllabic and phonemic complexity.* The primary factor considered was the articulatory ease of the response, e.g. monosyllabic utterances vs. bisyllabic utterances vs. multisyllabic utterances.

4. *Presence or absence of visual cues.* Stimulus material accompanied by visual cues elicits responses more easily than stimuli presented without visual cues.

5. *Presence or absence of auditory cues.* The presence or absence of contextual cues contained within a stimulus, e.g. sentence completion or questions with related words involved.

6. *Availability of a response.* A response's use in the English language was also considered carefully. High frequency words are elicited before low frequency words in the task hierarchy.

7. *Syntactic complexity of response.* High level stimulus material was developed to elicit responses with increasingly complex word order, use of additional parts of speech, e.g. prepositions, adjectives, adverbs, etc., and morphological components.

8. *Complexity of abstract concepts.* Some treatment stimulus material was selected to elicit the recall of infrequently used words, more complex constructions, and the expression of ideas.

It is suggested that the clinician also consider what he/she can do to control the task hierarchy. The clinician controlled variables include the following:

1. *Presence or Absence of Auditory Cues.* The clinician can repeat the stimulus, give additional information leading to the appropriate response, or provide phonemic cues.

2. *Presence or Absence of Visual Cues.* The clinician can use gestural cues or phonemic placement to elicit the appropriate response.

The verbal task hierarchy is theoretical and should not be implemented as an absolute progressive sequence of treatment for all patients. The clinician should develop a treatment protocol that progresses hierarchically, selecting those treatment tasks which are most appropriate for each individual patient. For example, a patient with "fluent" aphasia would probably find sentence completion tasks more difficult than responding to a question in which the response is contained within the stimulus.

It should be noted that many of the verbal tasks are applicable to the dysarthric and verbally apractic population and to cognitively impaired patients.

This section's major application to the dysarthric population lies

---

[1] Basso, A. Capitani, E. and Vignolo L.A.: Influence of rehabilitation on language skills in aphasic patients, *Arch Neurol, 36*:192, 1979.

in the "length of response" variable mentioned previously. Traditionally, a clinician teaches specific techniques to improve intelligibility (reduction of speaking rate, improved consonant precision, etc.). The patient begins by establishing success at the one syllable or word level and progresses to a multiple syllable or word level. Since length of response is the most carefully controlled variable in the verbal section, clinicians can use this section (Chaps. 1, 2, 3, and 5) to provide a stimulus task hierarchy for their dysarthric patients.

Application to the apraxic adult's rehabilitation is also possible because of the hierarchy's control for automaticity of response, length of response, and frequency of word use, which are major variables affecting the success of the apractic adult's verbal responses. The clinician may begin with highly facilitating tasks and progress to tasks that require less facilitation.

A large portion of Chapter 5 will be helpful material for the clinician working with cognitively impaired trauma patients, since it emphasizes expression of abstract concepts and encourages "thinking skills." The tasks in other chapters requiring categorization skills and responses to spatial and temporal questions are also applicable to this patient population.

SINGLE WORD RESPONSES

SINGLE WORD PRODUCTION—*IMITATIVE*

MATERIALS:	None.
TASK INSTRUCTIONS:	The clinician presents the stimulus, and the patient repeats it.
CLINICIAN INSTRUCTIONS:	"I'll say a word, and you say it after me. Watch me and listen carefully."
SUGGESTED CRITERIA:	None. Highly variable, and the clinician should establish the criteria for each patient.

(b)	(m)
BELL	ME
BYE	MY
BOY	MAY
BAY	MAN
BUN	MOM
BONE	MEAL
BOIL	MAT
BED	MILE
BOAT	MICE
BIKE	MEEK
(p)	(w)
PEA	WE
PIE	WHY
PAY	WAY
PAN	ONE
POOL	WALL
PIPE	WEED
PALM	WIN
PEAK	WOOL
PINE	WAIT
POT	WHEN

SINGLE WORD PRODUCTION—*IMITATIVE*

MATERIALS:	None.
TASK INSTRUCTIONS:	The clinician presents the stimulus, and the patient repeats it.
CLINICIAN INSTRUCTIONS:	"I'll say a word, and you say it after me. Watch me and listen carefully."
SUGGESTED CRITERIA:	None. Highly variable, and the clinician should establish the criteria for each patient.

(d)	(n)
DO	KNEE
DAY	NO
DIE	NEW
DOUGH	NOON
DAM	NAIL
DEEP	NEED
DIME	NIP
DID	NIGHT
DATE	NOSE
(t)	(l)
TEA	LIE
TOE	LEAP
TIE	LEG
TOY	LAY
TIME	LOOP
TEN	LAKE
TOOL	LINE
TIN	LET
TAIL	LOAD
TIGHT	LIGHT

SINGLE WORD PRODUCTION—*IMITATIVE*

MATERIALS:	None.
TASK INSTRUCTIONS:	The clinician presents the stimulus, and the patient repeats it.
CLINICIAN INSTRUCTIONS:	"I'll say a word, and you say it after me. Watch me and listen carefully."
SUGGESTED CRITERIA:	None. Highly variable, and the clinician should establish the criteria for each patient.

(k)	(g)
KEY	GO
CAN	GAY
CAT	GOAL
COOK	GOD
KILL	GALL
COAT	GOOD
KEEP	GUIDE
COOL	GAIN
COT	GATE
CAR	GOLD
(y)	**(h)**
YOU	HE
YELL	HIGH
YARN	HAT
YIELD	HEAP
YEN	HOT
YES	HATE
YEA	HILL
YOUNG	HOPE
YARD	HOOK
YOUTH	HOLE

SINGLE WORD PRODUCTION—*IMITATIVE*

MATERIALS:	None.
TASK INSTRUCTIONS:	The clinician presents the stimulus, and the patient repeats it.
CLINICIAN INSTRUCTIONS:	"I'll say a word, and you say it after me. Watch me and listen carefully."
SUGGESTED CRITERIA:	None. Highly variable, and the clinician should establish the criteria for each patient.

(s)	(z)
SEE	ZOO
SIGH	ZEAL
SAY	ZIP
SUN	ZERO
SELL	ZEST
SEED	ZONE
SIT	ZEBRA
SALE	ZOOM
SOUP	ZINC
SAT	ZAP
(th—voiced)	(th—unvoiced)
THE	THIGH
THEY	THINK
THOUGH	THANK
THAT	THOUGHT
THIS	THIN
THESE	THUMB
THEM	THIRD
THAN	THORN
THOSE	THEME
THEY	THICK

SINGLE WORD PRODUCTION—*IMITATIVE*

MATERIALS:	None.
TASK INSTRUCTIONS:	The clinician presents the stimulus, and the patient repeats it.
CLINICIAN INSTRUCTIONS:	"I'll say a word, and you say it after me. Watch me and listen carefully."
SUGGESTED CRITERIA:	None. Highly variable, and the clinician should establish the criteria for each patient.

(sh)	(ch)
SHE	CHEW
SHY	CHILD
SHOW	CHOSE
SHOE	CHIN
SHUT	CHOP
SHADE	CHEAT
SHAWL	CHILL
SHOP	CHIEF
SHAKE	CHASE
SHOUT	CHOICE
(j)	(r)
JOY	ROW
JUNE	ROT
JOKE	ROOK
JOB	REAP
JAM	RULE
JAIL	RAT
JEEP	RAKE
JET	RIGHT
JUICE	ROLL
JOIN	RAIL

SINGLE WORD PRODUCTION—*IMITATIVE*

MATERIALS:	None.
TASK INSTRUCTIONS:	The clinician presents the stimulus, and the patient repeats it.
CLINICIAN INSTRUCTIONS:	"I'll say a word, and you say it after me. Watch me and listen carefully."
SUGGESTED CRITERIA:	None. Highly variable, and the clinician should establish the criteria for each patient.

(f)	(v)
FEE	VIE
FOE	VEIL
FIGHT	VOTE
FOLD	VEAL
FALL	VOID
FOOT	VAT
FAIL	VIAL
FAR	VAN
FOOL	VINE
FOIL	VICE

(b—blends)	(t/th—blends)	(k—blends)
BLUE	TRY	CLOSE
BLIND	TREE	CLOWN
BLADE	TRIP	CLUE
BLEED	TRAIL	CLOCK
BLAME	TRAP	CRY
BROOM	THROUGH	CREEP
BRIGHT	THREE	CROSS
BRUSH	THROW	CREPE
BROIL	THRILL	QUIT
BRAT	THRONE	QUEEN

SINGLE WORD PRODUCTION—*IMITATIVE*

MATERIALS:	None.
TASK INSTRUCTIONS:	The clinician presents the stimulus, and the patient repeats it.
CLINICIAN INSTRUCTIONS:	"I'll say a word, and you say it after me. Watch me and listen carefully."
SUGGESTED CRITERIA:	None. Highly variable, and the clinician should establish the criteria for each patient.

(sm)	(sl)
SMALL	SLOW
SMOOTH	SLEEP
SMOKE	SLOT
SMOCK	SLIGHT
SMILE	SLAM
SMELL	SLAP
SMASH	SLOOP
SMOOCH	SLEEK
SMITE	SLIDE
SMUDGE	SLACKS
(st)	**(sk)**
STAY	SKY
STY	SCHOOL
STOP	SKIP
STEAL	SCAN
STOOP	SCALE
STAND	SKATE
STOLE	SKIN
STATE	SKIRT
STAMP	SKILL
STILL	SCOOP

SINGLE WORD SENTENCE COMPLETION—*AUTOMATIC*

MATERIALS: None.

TASK INSTRUCTIONS: Present stimulus items without
                           visual cues.

CLINICIAN INSTRUCTIONS: "I'll start a phrase, and you
                           finish it. Finish these phrases."

SUGGESTED CRITERIA: 80 percent accuracy without the
                           need for additional cues,
                           repetition of task instructions, or
                           significant delays in responding.

1. Up and_____.
2. Hot and_____.
3. Me and_____.
4. East and_____.
5. Stop and_____.
6. In and_____.
7. Black and_____.
8. Yes and_____.
9. Young and_____.
10. Cream and_____.
11. Salt and_____.
12. Night and_____.
13. Open and_____.
14. Left and_____.
15. Bread and_____.
16. Soap and_____.
17. Ice cream and_____.
18. Push and_____.
19. Over and_____.
20. Pen and_____.

SINGLE WORD SENTENCE COMPLETION—*AUTOMATIC*

MATERIALS: None.

TASK INSTRUCTIONS: Present stimulus items without visual cues.

CLINICIAN INSTRUCTIONS: "I'll start a phrase, and you finish it. Finish these phrases."

SUGGESTED CRITERIA: 80 percent accuracy without the need for additional cues, repetition of task instructions, or significant delays in responding.

1. North and_____.
2. White and_____.
3. Big and_____.
4. New and_____.
5. Wrong and_____.
6. On and_____.
7. Shirt and_____.
8. More or_____.
9. Paper and_____.
10. Nickels and_____.
11. A cup of_____.
12. Shoes and_____.
13. Peanut butter and_____.
14. His and_____.
15. Under and_____.
16. Doctor and_____.
17. Table and_____.
18. Hat and_____.
19. Dollars and_____.
20. Hammer and_____.

SINGLE WORD SENTENCE COMPLETION — *AUTOMATIC*

MATERIALS:	None.
TASK INSTRUCTIONS:	Present stimulus items without visual cues.
CLINICIAN INSTRUCTIONS:	"I'll start a sentence, and you finish it. Finish these sentences."
SUGGESTED CRITERIA:	80 percent accuracy without need for additional cues, repetition of task instructions, or significant delays in responding.

 1. Father and_____.
 2. Nickel and_____.
 3. Breakfast, lunch, and_____.
 4. Saturday and_____.
 5. One, two,_____.
 6. Red, white, and_____.
 7. Knife, fork, and_____.
 8. Man and_____.
 9. Boys and_____.
10. Husband and_____.
11. Monday, Tuesday,_____.
12. Now and_____.
13. Hands and_____.
14. Little by_____.
15. Here and_____.
16. Bacon and_____.
17. Cat and_____.
18. Brother and_____.
19. You and_____.
20. Good and_____.

SINGLE WORD SENTENCE COMPLETION—*AUTOMATIC*

MATERIALS:	None.
TASK INSTRUCTIONS:	Present stimulus items without visual cues.
CLINICIAN INSTRUCTIONS:	"I'll start a sentence and you finish it. Finish these sentences.
SUGGESTED CRITERIA:	80 percent accuracy without the need for additional cues, repetition of task instructions or significant delays in responding.

1. Don't cry over spilt_____.
2. The phone is off the_____.
3. It's raining cats and_____.
4. An apple a day keeps the doctor_____.
5. Early to bed, early to_____.
6. She was my teacher in the first_____.
7. It's on the tip of my_____.
8. Kill two birds with one_____.
9. All that glitters is not_____.
10. Brother, can you spare a_____.
11. It's as easy as_____.
12. She'll get here sooner or_____.
13. Clean as a_____.
14. Row, row, row your_____.
15. Look before you_____.
16. Turn over a new_____.
17. Humpty Dumpty sat on a_____.
18. That's neither here nor_____.
19. It's better to be safe than_____.
20. Too many cooks spoil the_____.

SINGLE WORD SENTENCE COMPLETION GIVEN VISUAL CUES

MATERIALS: A Pictures.

TASK INSTRUCTIONS: Arrange the stimulus items in two rows of five. When the criteria has been met, remove the visual cues and repeat the task.

CLINICIAN INSTRUCTIONS: "I'll start a sentence, and you finish it, using the name of one of these objects. Finish these sentences."

SUGGESTED CRITERIA: 90 percent accuracy without the presence of significant delays in responding or the need of additional cues.

1. You sit on a_____.
2. You tell time with a_____.
3. You drive a_____.
4. You drink from a_____.
5. You read a_____.
6. You fix hair with a_____.
7. You spend_____.
8. You eat soup with a_____.
9. Answer the_____.
10. You sleep in a_____.

SINGLE WORD SENTENCE COMPLETION GIVEN VISUAL CUES

MATERIALS: B Pictures.

TASK INSTRUCTIONS: Arrange the stimulus items on two rows of five. When the criteria has been met, remove the visual cues and repeat the task.

CLINICIAN INSTRUCTIONS: I'll start a sentence, and you finish it, using the name of one of these objects. Finish these sentences."

SUGGESTED CRITERIA: 90 percent accuracy without the presence of significant delays in responding or the need of additional cues.

1. You smoke a_____.
2. You ring a_____.
3. You fly a_____.
4. You cut wood with a_____.
5. When you go camping, you sleep under a_____.
6. You listen to the_____.
7. On a horse you put a_____.
8. In the rain, you open up your_____.
9. To see in the dark, you turn on your_____.
10. To keep food cold, you put it in the_____.

SINGLE WORD SENTENCE COMPLETION—*GIVEN VISUAL CUES*

MATERIALS:	C Pictures.
TASK INSTRUCTIONS:	Arrange the stimulus items in two rows of five. When the criteria has been met, remove the visual cues and repeat the task.
CLINICIAN INSTRUCTIONS:	"I'll start a sentence, and you finish it, using the name of one of these objects. Finish these sentences."
SUGGESTED CRITERIA:	90 percent accuracy without the presence of significant delays in responding or the need of additional cues.

1. You take a picture with a_____.
2. You weigh yourself on a_____.
3. You put a letter in an_____.
4. To find out the date, you look at the_____.
5. You fly in a_____.
6. You attach two pieces of paper together with a_____.
7. To make a flashlight run, you must put in some_____.
8. You cut your lawn with a_____.
9. You jump from a plane with a_____.
10. The fireman attaches his hose to the_____.

SINGLE WORD SENTENCE COMPLETION—*NOUNS*

MATERIALS:	None.
TASK INSTRUCTIONS:	Present stimulus items without visual cues.
CLINICIAN INSTRUCTIONS:	"I'll start a sentence, and you finish it. Finish these sentences."
SUGGESTED CRITERIA:	80 percent accuracy without the need for additional cues, repetition of task instructions, or significant delays in responding.

1. You eat a loaf of_____.
2. Drink a glass of_____.
3. You eat at the_____.
4. You live in a_____.
5. Put socks on your_____.
6. You cut with a_____.
7. Ring the_____.
8. You lock a door with a_____.
9. On your hands you have five_____.
10. Eat a piece of_____.
11. I want a cup of_____.
12. Put on your warm_____.
13. To see better, you put on your_____.
14. On Sunday some people go to_____.
15. Put on your socks and_____.
16. Don't forget to set the alarm_____.
17. You brush your teeth with a_____.
18. The little boy climbed up the_____.
19. I'll have a slice of bread and_____.
20. I have breakfast every_____.

SINGLE WORD SENTENCE COMPLETION—*NOUNS*

MATERIALS:	None.
TASK INSTRUCTIONS:	Present stimulus items without visual cues.
CLINICIAN INSTRUCTIONS:	"I'll start a sentence, and you finish it. Finish these sentences."
SUGGESTED CRITERIA:	80 percent accuracy without need for additional cues, repetition of task instructions, or significant delays in responding.

1. Comb your_____.
2. Shake my_____.
3. You smoke a_____.
4. You keep your pants up with a_____.
5. You write on a piece of_____.
6. It looks like it is going to_____.
7. You fly in a_____.
8. Open the_____.
9. Buy a dozen_____.
10. Wash the_____.
11. You cook in the_____.
12. Children go to_____.
13. Turn on the_____.
14. You pound nails with a_____.
15. On your head you wear a_____.
16. Put on your shoes and_____.
17. They own two cats and one_____.
18. She dove into the swimming_____.
19. To get to the roof he climbed up a_____.
20. People go skiing during the_____.

SINGLE WORD SENTENCE COMPLETION—*NOUNS*

MATERIALS: None.

TASK INSTRUCTIONS: Present stimulus items without visual cues.

CLINICIAN INSTRUCTIONS: "I'll start a sentence, and you finish it. Finish these sentences."

SUGGESTED CRITERIA: 80 percent accuracy without the need for additional cues, repetition of task instructions, or significant delays in responding.

 1. We went to a restaurant and ate_____.
 2. My brother has a_____.
 3. I will take the_____.
 4. The doctor will be_____.
 5. Will you have some_____.
 6. It's time to go to the_____.
 7. Where can I find the_____.
 8. I enjoy playing_____.
 9. The child is afraid of_____.
10. Did you find the_____.
11. They were sitting at the_____.
12. The deliveryman brought our_____.
13. The children are at the_____.
14. They bought a new_____.
15. My neighbor is planning a_____.
16. The lawn is much too_____.
17. The boy was carrying a_____.
18. The car had a broken_____.
19. The sky was full of_____.
20. We were late to the_____.

SINGLE WORD SENTENCE COMPLETION—*NOUNS*

MATERIALS: None.

TASK INSTRUCTIONS: Present stimulus items without visual cues.

CLINICIAN INSTRUCTIONS: "I'll start a sentence, and you finish it. Finish these sentences."

SUGGESTED CRITERIA: 80 percent accuracy without the need for additional cues, repetition of task instructions, or significant delays in responding.

1. Where did you get that_____.
2. When I go camping, I must remember the_____.
3. He had a good time at the_____.
4. I felt better after I_____.
5. Come right home after the_____.
6. I would like to go to the_____.
7. He couldn't eat all the_____.
8. The athlete was good at_____.
9. The lecture was about_____.
10. They couldn't fit in the_____.
11. Our children are at_____.
12. Make sure to bring your_____.
13. Put the dishes in the_____.
14. The animal was too_____.
15. It happened because the machine was_____.
16. He put the orange in the_____.
17. He tripped on the sidewalk because of the_____.
18. He was successful with his_____.
19. She took off her shoes because they were_____.
20. Make sure you have all the_____.

SINGLE WORD SENTENCE COMPLETION—*NOUNS*

MATERIALS:	None.
TASK INSTRUCTIONS:	Present stimulus items without visual cues.
CLINICIAN INSTRUCTIONS:	"I'll start a sentence, and you finish it. Finish these sentences."
SUGGESTED CRITERIA:	80 percent accuracy without the need for additional cues, repetition of task instructions, or significant delays in responding.

1. We were not interested in the_____.
2. We send cards to our_____.
3. They received a bill from their_____.
4. They plan to sell their_____.
5. Many people like to_____.
6. They were arguing about the_____.
7. I saw a picture of the_____.
8. The woman's hands felt_____.
9. The ribbon was very_____.
10. In the darkness, the dog looked like a_____.
11. Children often forget to wear_____.
12. The nurse will give me a_____.
13. Are you planning to take a_____.
14. Someday it would be nice to go to_____.
15. The bus was late because of the_____.
16. I need to buy a new pair of_____.
17. You bring the chicken, and I'll bring the_____.
18. The gardner forgot his_____.
19. Hang the pictures above the_____.
20. Stay home if you are_____.

SINGLE WORD SENTENCE COMPLETION—*NOUNS*

MATERIALS:	None.
TASK INSTRUCTIONS:	Present stimulus items without visual cues.
CLINICIAN INSTRUCTIONS:	"I'll start a sentence, and you finish it. Finish these sentences."
SUGGESTED CRITERIA:	80 percent accuracy without the need for additional cues, repetition of task instructions or significant delays in responding.

1. An agreement was made with the_____.
2. He ran out of patience with the_____.
3. The meeting was called to order by the_____.
4. They finished painting the house before it_____.
5. The game ended early because of the_____.
6. The package arrived before the_____.
7. Traffic was congested because of the_____.
8. The store was crowded because it was_____.
9. I had to wait a long time because it was_____.
10. I will go fishing if it is_____.
11. I plan on attending_____.
12. The newspaper headlines were_____.
13. The magazine article was about_____.
14. I will go shopping after I_____.
15. I had trouble with my_____.
16. There was a detour in the road because of the_____.
17. The repairman worked for hours on the_____.
18. I rode in the elevator to the_____.
19. The mountains were covered with_____.
20. I will go camping if I am_____.

SINGLE WORD SENTENCE COMPLETION— *VERBS*

MATERIALS: None.

TASK INSTRUCTIONS: Present stimulus items without visual cues.

CLINICIAN INSTRUCTIONS: "I'll start a sentence, and you finish it. Finish these sentences."

SUGGESTED CRITERIA: 80 percent accuracy without the need for additional cues, repetition of task instructions, or significant delays in responding.

1. Milk is for drinking, food is for_____.
2. Soap is for washing, a towel is for_____.
3. When we are happy we laugh, when we're sad we_____.
4. A crayon is for drawing, a pencil is for_____.
5. A spoon is for eating, a stove is for_____.
6. A mop is for mopping, a broom is for_____.
7. A stamp is for mailing, a book is for_____.
8. A chair is for sitting, a bed is for_____.
9. Matches are for lighting, a cigarette is for_____.
10. A bicycle is for riding, a car is for_____.
11. A nose is for smelling, eyes are for_____.
12. A mouth is for talking, ears are for_____.
13. A needle is for sewing, scissors are for_____.
14. A saw is for cutting, a hammer is for_____.
15. A letter is for sending, a telephone is for_____.
16. Bells are for ringing, voices are for_____.
17. Churches are for praying, schools are for_____.
18. Cats meow, dogs_____.
19. Horses run, elephants_____.
20. Monkeys climb, fish_____.

SINGLE WORD SENTENCE COMPLETION—*VERBS*

MATERIALS: None.

TASK INSTRUCTIONS: Present stimulus items without visual cues.

CLINICIAN INSTRUCTIONS: "I'll start a sentence, and you finish it. Finish these sentences."

SUGGESTED CRITERIA: 80 percent accuracy without the need for additional cues, repetition of task instructions, or significant delays in responding.

1. Money is for_____.
2. Pens are for_____.
3. Keys are for_____.
4. Newspapers are for_____.
5. Scissors are for_____.
6. Glasses are for_____.
7. A needle and thread are for_____.
8. A fork is for_____.
9. Soap is for_____.
10. Schools are for_____.
11. Hammers are for_____.
12. Planes are for_____.
13. Brooms are for_____.
14. Balls are for_____.
15. Televisions are for_____.
16. Kites are for_____.
17. Razors are for_____.
18. Bicycles are for_____.
19. Letters are for_____.
20. Noses are for_____.

SINGLE WORD SENTENCE COMPLETION — *VERBS*

MATERIALS: None.

TASK INSTRUCTIONS: Present stimulus items without
           visual cues.

CLINICIAN INSTRUCTIONS: "I'll start a sentence, and you
           finish it. Finish these sentences."

SUGGESTED CRITERIA: 80 percent accuracy without the
           need for additional cues,
           repetition of task instructions, or
           significant delays in responding.

1. Ladders are for_____.
2. Shovels are for_____.
3. Stairs are for_____.
4. Ears are for_____.
5. Hangers are for_____.
6. Clocks are for_____.
7. Clothes are for_____.
8. Bows are for_____.
9. Buttons are for_____.
10. Toys are for_____.
11. Straws are for_____.
12. Balloons are for_____.
13. Music is for_____.
14. Stones are for_____.
15. Cameras are for_____.
16. Windows are for_____.
17. Yardsticks are for_____.
18. Books are for_____.
19. Horns are for_____.
20. Hair is for_____.

SINGLE WORD RESPONSE—*RESPONSE PROVIDED IN STIMULI*

MATERIALS:	None.
TASK INSTRUCTIONS:	Present stimulus items without visual cues.
CLINICIAN INSTRUCTIONS:	"I'm going to ask you a question, and you answer it."
SUGGESTED CRITERIA:	100 percent accuracy without need for additional cues, repetition of task instructions, or significant delays in responding.

WHICH DO YOU LIKE BETTER—
1. Soda or milk?
2. Cake or bread?
3. Red or blue?
4. Dogs or cats?
5. Coffee or tea?
6. Rain or snow?
7. Jam or jelly?
8. Boys or girls?
9. Apples or oranges?
10. Brushes or combs?
11. Peas or beans?
12. Soup or salad?
13. T.V. or radio?
14. Pens or pencils?
15. Juice or soda?
16. Lakes or rivers?
17. Cigars or pipes?
18. Cookies or pie?
19. Hills or valleys?
20. Summer or winter?

SINGLE WORD RESPONSE—*RESPONSE PROVIDED IN STIMULI*

MATERIALS: None.

TASK INSTRUCTIONS: Present stimulus items without visual cues.

CLINICIAN INSTRUCTIONS: "I'm going to ask you a question, and you answer it."

SUGGESTED CRITERIA: 100 percent accuracy without need for additional cues, repetition of task instructions, or significant delays in responding.

WHICH DO YOU LIKE BETTER—
1. Pants or skirts?
2. Baths or showers?
3. The South or the North?
4. Running or walking?
5. Butter or margarine?
6. Gold or silver?
7. Working or sleeping?
8. Juice or cola?
9. Cooking or eating?
10. Chocolate or vanilla?
11. Laughing or crying?
12. Mountains or oceans?
13. Leather or plastic?
14. Swimming or sunning?
15. Talking or listening?
16. Newspapers or magazines?
17. Brunettes or blonds?
18. California or Illinois?
19. To be late or early?
20. Messiness or neatness?

SINGLE WORD RESPONSE—*RESPONSE PROVIDED IN STIMULI*

MATERIALS:	A and B Words.
TASK INSTRUCTIONS:	Arrange stimulus items in two rows of five. Clinician points to each stimulus as he/she asks the questions.
CLINICIAN INSTRUCTIONS:	"I'm going to ask you a question about each of these, and you answer it."
SUGGESTED CRITERIA:	90 percent accuracy without the need for additional cues, repetition of task instructions, or significant delays in responding.

A WORDS
  1. (Book): Is this a book or a lamp?
  2. (Spoon): Is this a plate or a spoon?
  3. (Bed): Is this a chair or a bed?
  4. (Brush): Is this a glass or a brush?
  5. (Phone): Is this a phone or a watch?
  6. (Money): Is this a purse or money?
  7. (Chair): Is this a table or a chair?
  8. (Cup): Is this a saucer or a cup?
  9. (Watch): Is this a watch or a comb?
 10. (Car): Is this a car or a plane?

B WORDS
 11. (Kite): Is this a kite or a bird?
 12. (Pipe): Is this a brush or a pipe?
 13. (Saw): Is this a hammer or a saw?
 14. (Radio): Is this a T.V. or a radio?
 15. (Tent): Is this a tent or a house?
 16. (Bell): Is this a bell or an envelope?
 17. (Saddle): Is this a horse or a saddle?
 18. (Umbrella): Is this a hat or an umbrella?
 19. (Flashlight): Is this a flashlight or a lamp?
 20. (Refrigerator): Is this a refrigerator or a stove?

SINGLE WORD RESPONSE—*RESPONSE PROVIDED IN STIMULI*

MATERIALS:	None.
TASK INSTRUCTIONS:	Present stimulus items without visual cues.
CLINICIAN INSTRUCTIONS:	"I'm going to ask you a question, and you answer it."
SUGGESTED CRITERIA:	100 percent accuracy without need for additional cues, repetition of task instructions, or significant delays in responding.

1. Who takes care of sick people—a nurse or a gardener?
2. Which smells good—skunks or flowers?
3. Which one bites—a snake or a worm?
4. When do people go to church—on Sunday or Tuesday?
5. Which should you eat when losing weight—cake or carrots?
6. Which one makes you laugh—a clown or a teacher?
7. Which one makes more noise—a tiger or a kitten?
8. Which tells you the date—a picture or a calendar?
9. Who rules the country—a president or a judge?
10. Which tastes better—grapes or marbles?
11. Who types for a living—a cook or a secretary?
12. Which do you eat—plates or toast?
13. Where do we sleep—in a bedroom or a bathroom?
14. Which do you find in a pen—ink or lead?
15. Which do you listen to—a rug or a violin?
16. Which can you see outside—grass or beds?
17. Which can you drink from—a lamp or a bottle?
18. Which do you blow your nose with—a tissue or a dress?
19. Which do you read—a magazine or a drawer?
20. Which do you mail—a pencil or an envelope?

SINGLE WORD RESPONSE—*RESPONSE PROVIDED IN STIMULI*

MATERIALS:	None.
TASK INSTRUCTIONS:	Present stimulus items without visual cues.
CLINICIAN INSTRUCTIONS:	"I'm going to ask you a question, and you answer it."
SUGGESTED CRITERIA:	100 percent accuracy without need for additional cues, repetition of task instructions, or significant delays in responding.

1. What do you listen to—a radio or a book?
2. Which is bigger—a nail or a pin?
3. What do you read—a box or a newspaper?
4. Which one rings—a cup or a bell?
5. Where do we swim—in a pool or a bed?
6. Which one gives time—a clock or a picture?
7. Who sells pastry—a butcher or a baker?
8. When do we eat breakfast—morning or night?
9. Where do we buy food—in a hardware store or a grocery?
10. Who gives shots—a nurse or a clerk?
11. When do we go to bed—in the morning or night?
12. What animal eats bananas—a monkey or a giraffe?
13. Who directs traffic—a doctor or a policeman?
14. Which one delivers mail—a mailman or a milkman?
15. When do the leaves start coming out—the winter or the spring?
16. When do we see snow—in the summer or winter?
17. Which is sour—a grapefruit or a plum?
18. Where do you cook—in a kitchen or a bedroom?
19. Who eats more—a mouse or an elephant?
20. Which is sharper—a razor or a knife?

SINGLE WORD RESPONSE—*RESPONSE PROVIDED IN STIMULI*

MATERIALS:	None.
TASK INSTRUCTIONS:	Present stimulus items without visual cues.
CLINICIAN INSTRUCTIONS:	"I'm going to ask you a question, and you answer it."
SUGGESTED CRITERIA:	100 percent accuracy without need for additional cues, repetition of task instructions or delays in responding.

1. Which do you sit in—a chair or a table?
2. Which do you watch—a T.V. or a radio?
3. Which do you eat—music or food?
4. Which do you drink—coffee or wood?
5. Which do you sleep on—a bed or a table?
6. Which do you eat with—a watch or a fork?
7. Which do you write with—glasses or a pencil?
8. Who takes care of you—a doctor or a mailman?
9. Who wears a dress—a man or a woman?
10. Which do you ride in—a train or a bed?
11. Which do you turn on—a radio or a book?
12. Which do you lock with—a watch or a key?
13. Which do you wear around your waist—a belt or a hat?
14. Which do you swim in—water or milk?
15. Which do you read—a book or a T.V.?
16. Which do you put on eggs—salt or sugar?
17. Which do you fix hair with—glasses or a comb?
18. Which do you wear on your feet—shoes or gloves?
19. Which do you see with—your ears or your eyes?
20. Which do you live in—a house or a plane?

SINGLE WORD PRODUCTION—*RESPONSE PROVIDED IN STIMULI*

MATERIALS:	None.
TASK INSTRUCTIONS:	Present stimulus items without visual cues.
CLINICIAN INSTRUCTIONS:	"I'm going to say a sentence and then ask you a question about that sentence."
SUGGESTED CRITERIA:	90 percent accuracy without the need for additional cues, repetition of task instructions, or significant delays in responding.

The cat ate the fish.
    1. Who ate?
    2. What did the cat eat?
The dentist filled the tooth with gold.
    3. Who filled the tooth?
    4. What did he fill it with?
The father watched the child playing.
    5. Who watched the child?
    6. What was the child doing?
My sister was eating soup.
    7. Who was eating?
    8. What was she eating?
Joan spilled the ink.
    9. Who spilled?
    10. What did she spill?
The teacher taught math.
    11. Who taught?
    12. What did he teach?
The chef baked a cake.
    13. Who baked?
    14. What did he bake?
My aunt watches T.V.
    15. Who watches?
    16. What does she watch?

The neighbors ski in March.

    17. Who goes in March?

    18. What do they do in March?

The girls listen to the radio.

    19. Who listens?

    20. What do they listen to?

SINGLE WORD PRODUCTION—*RESPONSE PROVIDED IN STIMULI*

MATERIALS:	None.
TASK INSTRUCTIONS:	Present stimulus items without visual cues.
CLINICIAN INSTRUCTIONS:	"I'm going to say a sentence and then ask you a question about that sentence."
SUGGESTED CRITERIA:	90 percent accuracy without the need for additional cues, repetition of task instructions, or significant delays in responding.

The dog wagged his tail.
1. Who wagged?
2. What did he wag?
The mailman delivers the mail.
3. Who delivered?
4. What did he deliver?
The man looked at his watch.
5. Who looked?
6. What did he look at?
The tree was in the yard.
7. What was in the yard?
8. Where was the tree?
The bacon tasted bad.
9. What tasted bad?
10. How did the bacon taste?
The house was blue.
11. What was blue?
12. What color was the house?
The nurse put the picture in her purse.
13. Who put it in?
14. Where did she put it?
My uncle washed the dishes in the sink.
15. Who washed the dishes?
16. Where did he wash them?

Mother waved her hand at the policeman.

    17. Who waved her hand?

    18. Who did she wave to?

The mouse ran across the floor.

    19. Who ran?

    20. What did he run across?

SINGLE WORD RESPONSE—*RECALLING NOUNS WITH VISUAL CUES*

MATERIALS: A Pictures.

TASK INSTRUCTIONS: Place the pictures on the table, one at a time. Elicit the name of each object by providing the object's function in question form. When the criteria has been met, remove the auditory stimuli and ask the patient to name the pictures.

CLINICIAN INSTRUCTIONS: "I'll ask you a question, and you answer it."

SUGGESTED CRITERIA: 90 percent accuracy without the presence of significant delays in responding or the need for additional cues.

1. (Car): What do we ride in?
2. (Watch): What do we tell time with?
3. (Phone): What do we call people on?
4. (Bed): What do we sleep in?
5. (Brush): What do we fix hair with?
6. (Money): What do we spend?
7. (Chair): What do we sit on?
8. (Book): What do we read?
9. (Spoon): What do we stir with?
10. (Cup): What do we drink coffee from?

SINGLE WORD RESPONSE—*RECALLING NOUNS WITH VISUAL CUES*

MATERIALS:	B Pictures.
TASK INSTRUCTIONS:	Place the pictures on the table, one at a time. Elicit the name of each object by providing the object's function in question form. When the criteria has been met, remove the auditory stimuli and ask the patient to name the pictures.
CLINICIAN INSTRUCTIONS:	"I'll ask a question, and you answer it."
SUGGESTED CRITERIA:	90 percent accuracy without the presence of significant delays in responding or the need for additional cues.

1. (Bell): What do you ring?
2. (Pipe): What do you smoke?
3. (Saw): What do you cut wood with?
4. (Kite): What do you fly in the wind?
5. (Tent): What do you sleep under when you go camping?
6. (Saddle): What do you put on a horse?
7. (Radio): What do you turn on and listen to?
8. (Umbrella): What do you open up to protect yourself from the rain?
9. (Refrigerator): Where do you put food to keep it cold?
10. (Flashlight): What do you turn on to see in the dark?

SINGLE WORD RESPONSE—*RECALLING NOUNS WITH VISUAL CUES*

MATERIALS:	C Pictures.
TASK INSTRUCTIONS:	Place the pictures on the table, one at a time. Elicit the name of each object by providing the object's function in question form. When the criteria has been met, remove the auditory stimuli and ask the patient to name the pictures.
CLINICIAN INSTRUCTIONS:	"I'll ask you a question, and you answer it."
SUGGESTED CRITERIA:	90 percent accuracy without the presence of significant delays in responding or the need for additional cues.

1. (Scale): What do you weigh yourself on?
2. (Camera): What do you take pictures with?
3. (Envelope): What do you put a letter in?
4. (Calendar): What do you look at to find the date?
5. (Stapler): What do you attach two pieces of paper together with?
6. (Helicopter): What do you fly in?
7. (Battery): What do you put in a flashlight to make it run?
8. (Parachute): What do you use when jumping from a plane?
9. (Lawn mower): What do you cut your lawn with?
10. (Fire hydrant): What does a fireman attach his hose to?

SINGLE WORD RESPONSE—*RECALLING COMMON NOUNS*

MATERIALS: None.

TASK INSTRUCTIONS: Present stimulus items without visual cues.

CLINICIAN INSTRUCTIONS: "I'm going to ask you a question, and you answer it."

SUGGESTED CRITERIA: 90 percent accuracy without the need for additional cues, repetition of task instructions, or significant delays in responding.

1. What does a baby drink?
2. What do you fix hair with?
3. What do you fly in?
4. What do you drink out of?
5. What do you read?
6. What do you lock a door with?
7. What do you call people on?
8. What do you drive?
9. What do you wear on your feet?
10. What do we sit on?
11. What do you tell time with?
12. What do you write with?
13. What do you pick up food with?
14. What do you wear on your head?
15. What do we sleep in?
16. What do we sweeten coffee with?
17. What do you drink?
18. What do you row in the water?
19. What do we spread on bread?
20. What is in the sky that is hot?

SINGLE WORD RESPONSE—*RECALLING VERBS*

MATERIALS: None.

TASK INSTRUCTIONS: Present stimulus items without visual cues.

CLINICIAN INSTRUCTIONS: "I'm going to ask you a question, and you answer it."

SUGGESTED CRITERIA: 90 percent accuracy without the need for additional cues, repetition of task instructions, or significant delays in responding.

1. What do logs do in the fireplace?
2. What do you do in a restaurant?
3. What do you do with your eyes?
4. What do you do in the kitchen?
5. What do you do with a ball?
6. What do you do with a chair?
7. What do you do in a swimming pool?
8. What do you do with a pencil?
9. What do you do with your ears?
10. What do you do with a car?
11. What do you do with a cigarette?
12. What do you do with a radio?
13. What do you do with a T.V.?
14. What do you do with a table?
15. What do you do with water?
16. What do you do with money?
17. What do you do with a door bell?
18. What does the sun do?
19. What does a baby do?
20. What does ice do when you hold it in your hand?

SINGLE WORD RESPONSE—*RECALLING PLACES*

MATERIALS: None.

TASK INSTRUCTIONS: Present stimulus items without visual cues.

CLINICIAN INSTRUCTIONS: "I'm going to ask you a question, and you answer it."

SUGGESTED CRITERIA: 90 percent accuracy without the need for additional cues, repetition of task instructions, or significant delays in responding.

1. Where do we buy food?
2. Where do children go to learn?
3. Where do people pray?
4. Where do we buy gas?
5. Where do we buy stamps?
6. Where do we buy clothes?
7. Where do we go for surgery?
8. Where do we stay at night, in a strange city?
9. Where do we buy sandpaper and tools?
10. Where do we go to eat out?
11. Where would you buy a birthday cake?
12. Where do you wash clothes if you don't own a washing machine?
13. What is America's coldest state?
14. What is America's largest state?
15. What country is directly above us?
16. What country is directly below us?
17. In what room do we eat dinner?
18. In what room do we sleep?
19. In what room do you cook food?
20. Where do you house a car?

SINGLE WORD RESPONSE—*RECALLING TEMPORAL WORDS*

MATERIALS:	None.
TASK INSTRUCTIONS:	Present stimulus items without visual cues.
CLINICIAN INSTRUCTIONS:	"I'm going to ask you a question, and you answer it."
SUGGESTED CRITERIA:	90 percent accuracy without the need for additional cues, repetition of task instructions, or significant delays in responding.

1. When do we eat breakfast?
2. When do we eat dinner?
3. In which season does the snow fall?
4. Which is the hottest season?
5. In which season do the leaves start falling?
6. In which season do the leaves start coming out?
7. What month is Christmas in?
8. What month is Thanksgiving in?
9. In which month is Washington's and Lincoln's birthdays?
10. In what month is New Year's Day?
11. In which month is your birthday?
12. When do children go trick or treating?
13. What day do some people go to church?
14. What year were you born in?
15. What year is this?
16. During what holiday do we give and receive presents?
17. During what holiday do we have a big turkey dinner?
18. When do children come home from school?
19. What month is this?
20. What day of the week is it?

SINGLE WORD RESPONSE—*RECALLING PEOPLE*

MATERIALS:	None.
TASK INSTRUCTIONS:	Present stimulus items without visual cues.
CLINICIAN INSTRUCTIONS:	"I'm going to ask you a question, and you answer it."
SUGGESTED CRITERIA:	90 percent accuracy without the need for additional cues, repetition of task instructions, or significant delays in responding.

1. Who flies planes?
2. Who puts out fires?
3. Who delivers mail?
4. Who enforces the law?
5. Who teaches children in school?
6. Who delivers milk?
7. Who fixes your teeth?
8. Who argues cases in court?
9. Who prescribes medicines and diagnoses illnesses?
10. Who takes your blood pressure and temperature?
11. Who runs the country?
12. Whom do we hire to care for our children when we go out?
13. Whom does a young child believe brings Christmas presents?
14. Who discovered America?
15. Who is our president?
16. Who was the first president of the United States?
17. Who celebrates Hanukkah?
18. Which president freed the slaves?
19. What people were in this country before the white man came?
20. Who treats mental problems?

SINGLE WORD RESPONSE—*RECALLING DIFFICULT NOUNS*

MATERIALS:	None.
TASK INSTRUCTIONS:	Present stimulus items without visual cues.
CLINICIAN INSTRUCTIONS:	"I'm going to ask you a question, and you answer it."
SUGGESTED CRITERIA:	90 percent accuracy without the need for additional cues, repetition of task instructions, or significant delays in responding.

1. What do you call the list of foods presented you in a restaurant?
2. In which state do people wear ten-gallon hats?
3. Which animal has a long trunk?
4. Which animal has black and white stripes?
5. What do you call the last car on a train?
6. What do you call the first car on a train?
7. What do we call the object that displays the months, weeks, and days of the year?
8. What do we cut the grass with?
9. What bird do we eat at Thanksgiving?
10. What's at the end of a pencil?
11. Which animal sees in the dark and hoots?
12. What do some people put on hot dogs? hamburgers?
13. What do we measure with?
14. Which insect makes a web?
15. What do you call the whiskers on a man's upper lip?
16. What do we put in our mouths to take temperatures?
17. What do we call the succulent plant found in the desert?
18. Which animal gives off a bad odor for protection?
19. What do you call the precious gem that most engagement rings have?
20. What do we cover a cut with?

SINGLE WORD RESPONSE—*RECALL OF CATEGORY MEMBERS*

MATERIALS: None.

TASK INSTRUCTIONS: Present stimulus items without visual cues.

CLINICIAN INSTRUCTIONS: "I want you to name some things from various categories."

SUGGESTED CRITERIA: 90 percent accuracy without the need for additional cues, repetition of task instructions, or significant delays in responding.

1. Name something to drink.
2. Name something to eat.
3. Name an animal.
4. Name a color.
5. Name an article of clothing.
6. Name a state.
7. Name a month.
8. Name a day of the week.
9. Name a tool.
10. Name a fruit.
11. Name a vegetable.
12. Name something sweet.
13. Name something hot.
14. Name something sour.
15. Name something cold.
16. Name something green.
17. Name something white.
18. Name something very small.
19. Name something very big.
20. Name a country.

SINGLE WORD RESPONSE— *RECALL OF CATEGORY MEMBERS*

MATERIALS: None.

TASK INSTRUCTIONS: Present stimulus items without
                              visual cues.

CLINICIAN INSTRUCTIONS: "I want you to name some
                              things from various categories."

SUGGESTED CRITERIA: 90 percent accuracy without the
                              need for additional cues,
                              repetition of task instructions, or
                              significant delays in responding.

1. Name something that is sticky.
2. Name something that is wet.
3. Name something that is long.
4. Name something that is slow.
5. Name something that is soft.
6. Name something that is expensive.
7. Name something that is heavy.
8. Name something that is sharp.
9. Name something that is fast.
10. Name something that is hard.
11. Name something that is electric.
12. Name something that is shiny.
13. Name something that is lightweight.
14. Name something that is good smelling.
15. Name something that is carbonated.
16. Name something that is cheap.
17. Name something that is round.
18. Name something that is square.
19. Name something that is plastic.
20. Name something that is made of metal.

SINGLE WORD RESPONSE—*RECALL OF CATEGORIES*

MATERIALS: None.

TASK INSTRUCTIONS: Stimulus presented without
                            visual cues.

CLINICIAN INSTRUCTIONS: "I'll say three words, and you
                            tell me to what category they
                            belong. _____,
                            _____, and
                            _____ are all. . . ."

SUGGESTED CRITERIA: 90 percent accuracy without the
                            presence of significant delays in
                            responding or the need for
                            additional cues.

1. Elephants, tigers, and dogs.
2. Pants, skirts, and socks.
3. Tables, chairs, and beds.
4. Blue, red, and green.   •
5. Meat, vegetables, and fruit.
6. Hammer, screwdriver, and wrench.
7. March, June, and December.
8. Five, three, and twelve.
9. Milk, water, and juice.
10. Apples, bananas, and peaches.
11. German sheperds, collies, and golden retrievers.
12. Pigeons, sparrows, and blue jays.
13. Peas, beans, and spinach.
14. Sharks, tuna, and salmon.
15. Ring, bracelet, and necklace.
16. Schools, banks, and stores.
17. Illinois, California, and Florida.
18. Lincoln, Washington, and Kennedy.
19. France, England, and the United States.
20. Angry, sad, and happy.

TWO AND THREE WORD RESPONSES

TWO AND THREE WORD RESPONSES—
NO SYNTACTIC RESTRICTIONS

MATERIALS: None.

TASK INSTRUCTIONS: Present stimulus items without
                        visual cues.

CLINICIAN INSTRUCTIONS: "I want you to name some
                        things from various categories."

SUGGESTED CRITERIA: 90 percent accuracy without the
                        need for additional cues,
                        repetition of task instructions, or
                        significant delays in responding.

NAME TWO OR THREE—
 1. Sports.
 2. Foods.
 3. Animals.
 4. Articles of clothing.
 5. Furniture.
 6. Liquids.
 7. Fruits.
 8. Vegetables.
 9. States.
10. Countries.
11. Cities.
12. Sweets.
13. Musical instruments.
14. Modes of transportation.
15. Precious gems.
16. Tools.
17. Colors.
18. Months.
19. Female names.
20. Male names.

TWO AND THREE WORD RESPONSES—
NO SYNTACTIC RESTRICTIONS

MATERIALS: None.

TASK INSTRUCTIONS: Present stimulus items without visual cues.

CLINICIAN INSTRUCTIONS: "I want you to name some things from various categories."

SUGGESTED CRITERIA: 90 percent accuracy without the need for additional cues, repetition of task instructions, or significant delays in responding.

NAME TWO OR THREE—
1. Things that are expensive.
2. Things that swim.
3. Things that are in a newspaper.
4. Things that you smoke.
5. Things that are hot.
6. Things that are cold.
7. Things that are electric.
8. Things that are lightweight.
9. Things that are good smelling.
10. Things that are green.
11. Things that you can read.
12. Things that you can move.
13. Things that you can fly.
14. Things that are made of metal.
15. Things that are square.
16. Things that make a noise.
17. Things that are sour.
18. Things that have a bad odor.
19. Things that you can listen to.
20. Things that are shiny.

TWO AND THREE WORD RESPONSES—*NO SYNTACTIC RESTRICTIONS*

MATERIALS: None.

TASK INSTRUCTIONS: Present stimulus items without visual cues.

CLINICIAN INSTRUCTIONS: "I'm going to have you name some things."

SUGGESTED CRITERIA: 90 percent accuracy without the need for additional cues, repetition of task instructions, or significant delays in responding.

NAME TWO OR THREE—
1. Things to make a sandwich with.
2. Things you find in a drugstore.
3. Things you find in a hall closet.
4. Things you can wash.
5. Things that are soft.
6. Things that can roll.
7. Things that are carbonated.
8. Western states.
9. Eastern states.
10. Large cities.
11. National holidays.
12. Professions.
13. Things you find in a bakery.
14. Things you would find in Africa.
15. Things that can be found in tin cans.
16. Things you find in an ocean.
17. Religions.
18. Kinds of weather.
19. Kinds of boats.
20. Kinds of pills we take.

TWO AND THREE WORD RESPONSES—
NO SYNTACTIC RESTRICTIONS

MATERIALS: None.

TASK INSTRUCTIONS: Present stimulus items without visual cues.

CLINICIAN INSTRUCTIONS: "I'm going to have you name some things."

SUGGESTED CRITERIA: 90 percent accuracy without the need for additional cues, repetition of task instructions, or significant delays in responding.

1. What do you need in order to write a letter?
2. What do you need in order to mail a letter?
3. What do you need to make chocolate milk?
4. What are the weekend days?
5. What are the winter months?
6. What are the summer months?
7. What color can an apple be?
8. What do you need in order to make a cheese omelette?
9. What do you need in order to wash dishes?
10. What do you need in order to go fishing?
11. What do you need in order to pop popcorn?
12. What are the colors of the American flag?
13. What are the warmest seasons?
14. For what occasions might we buy presents for people?
15. What do you need to change diapers?
16. What medical people take care of you when you are sick?
17. What are the three primary subjects taught in school?
18. What animals are most often kept as house pets?
19. What food is served at birthday parties?
20. What two things do you wear on your feet?

TWO AND THREE WORD RESPONSES—
NO SYNTACTIC RESTRICTIONS

MATERIALS: None.

TASK INSTRUCTIONS: Present stimulus items without visual cues.

CLINICIAN INSTRUCTIONS: "I'm going to have you name some things."

SUGGESTED CRITERIA: 90 percent accuracy without the need for additional cues, repetition of task instructions, or significant delays in responding.

1. What do you need to take a picture?
2. What are the three meals of the day?
3. What two things do you season eggs with?
4. What utensils do you eat with?
5. What do you need to sweep the floor?
6. What do you need to make ice?
7. What do you need to make a fire?
8. What do you need to brush your teeth?
9. What do you need to make toast?
10. What can people put in their coffee?
11. What do you need to wash your face?
12. What things do people smoke?
13. What three colors are seen on stoplights?
14. What are the three most popular ball sports?
15. What are the political parties?
16. What things do you find on a bed?
17. What things do you need in order to sew on a button?
18. What are the fall months?
19. What are three primary modes of transportation?
20. What usually accompanies an electric storm?

PHRASE PRODUCTION—*RESPONSE PROVIDED IN STIMULUS*

MATERIALS:	None.
TASK INSTRUCTIONS:	Present stimulus items without visual cues.
CLINICIAN INSTRUCTIONS:	"I'm going to say a sentence, and then I will ask you questions about the sentence."
SUGGESTED CRITERIA:	90 percent accuracy without the need for additional cues, repetition of task instructions, or significant delays in responding.

Tomorrow morning I'm going shopping with my mother.
    1. What am I going to do with my mother?
    2. When am I going?
Last night, I had a good home-cooked meal.
    3. When did I have this meal?
    4. What did I have last night?
The old man read his newspaper every morning.
    5. What did he do?
    6. How often did he read it?
My next-door neighbors are leaving in the morning.
    7. When are they going to leave?
    8. Who is going to leave?
We sat on the front porch watching the cars go by.
    9. Where did we sit?
    10. What did we do there?
She watered the plants that were in the downstairs bedroom.
    11. Where did she water the plants?
    12. What did she do?
Tim yelled at the children who were making noise in the yard.
    13. What were the children doing?
    14. What did Tim do?
Yesterday afternoon, I watched Sandy sing.
    15. What did I do?
    16. When did I watch her sing?
He saw two white bears at the New York Zoo.
    17. What did he see?

18. Where did he see them?

A university professor wrote an article about the rising costs of living.

19. Who wrote the story?
20. What was the article about?

PHRASE PRODUCTION—*RESPONSE PROVIDED IN STIMULUS*

MATERIALS: None.

TASK INSTRUCTIONS: Present stimulus items without visual cues.

CLINICIAN INSTRUCTIONS: "I'm going to say a sentence, and then I will ask you questions about the sentence."

SUGGESTED CRITERIA: 90 percent accuracy without the need for additional cues, significant delays in responding, or errors of syntax and grammar.

Yesterday afternoon, we bought two blue chairs.
1. What did we buy?
2. When did we buy them?

I watched the ducks in his father's pond.
3. Where were the ducks?
4. What did I do there?

She spilt the juice on her mother's living room rug.
5. Where was the spill?
6. What did she do?

My father lost all his money during the war.
7. What did my father do?
8. When did he lose his money?

I bought a book about flowers on the west coast.
9. What did I do?
10. What was the book about?

His father-in-law was angry about the work done on the fence.
11. Who was angry?
12. What was he angry about?

Roses and daisies grew in the lot next door.
13. What grew?
14. Where did they grow?

Children's furniture can be found on the second and third floors.
15. What can be found?
16. Where can it be found?

The boss' daughter came to see if her father was done.

17. Who came?
18. Why did she come?

Skirts and sweaters are worn during the fall season.

19. What are worn?
20. When are they worn?

PHRASE PRODUCTION—*STATING FUNCTIONS OF OBJECTS*

MATERIALS: A and B Pictures.

TASK INSTRUCTIONS: Place a picture card on the
                              table, and ask the patient it's
                              function.

CLINICIAN INSTRUCTIONS: "I'll show you a picture of an
                              object, and you tell me what
                              you do with it."

SUGGESTED CRITERIA: 90 percent accuracy without the
                              need for additional cues,
                              significant delays in responding,
                              or errors of syntax and
                              grammar.

WHAT DO YOU DO WITH A—
 1. Watch.
 2. Chair.
 3. Spoon.
 4. Bed.
 5. Book.
 6. Car.
 7. Phone.
 8. Brush.
 9. Money.
10. Cup.
11. Radio.
12. Pipe.
13. Kite.
14. Saw.
15. Tent.
16. Refrigerator.
17. Flashlight.
18. Saddle.
19. Umbrella.
20. Bell.

PHRASE PRODUCTION—*STATING FUNCTIONS OF OBJECTS*

MATERIALS: C Pictures.

TASK INSTRUCTIONS: Place a picture card on the table, and ask the patient it's function.

CLINICIAN INSTRUCTIONS: "I'll show you a picture of an object, and you tell me what you do with it."

SUGGESTED CRITERIA: 90 percent accuracy without the need for additional cues, significant delays in responding, or errors of syntax and grammar.

WHAT DO YOU DO WITH A—
1. Calendar.
2. Helicopter.
3. Lawn mower.
4. Fire hydrant.
5. Stapler.
6. Battery.
7. Camera.
8. Scale.
9. Parachute.
10. Envelope.

PHRASE PRODUCTION—*STATING FUNCTIONS OF OBJECTS*

MATERIALS: None.

TASK INSTRUCTIONS: Present stimulus items without visual cue.

CLINICIAN INSTRUCTIONS: "I'll say the name of an object, and you tell me what you do with it."

SUGGESTED CRITERIA: 90 percent accuracy without the need for additional cues, significant delays in responding, or errors of syntax and grammar.

WHAT DO YOU DO WITH (A)—
1. Sugar.
2. Sink.
3. Shoes and socks.
4. Butter.
5. Matches.
6. Window.
7. Salt.
8. Washing machine.
9. Wallet.
10. Sweater.
11. Needle.
12. Hammer.
13. Glass.
14. Paper.
15. Hanger.
16. Vase.
17. Handkerchief.
18. Newspaper.
19. Lamp.
20. Key.

PHRASE PRODUCTION—*STATING FUNCTIONS OF OBJECTS*

MATERIALS:	None.
TASK INSTRUCTIONS:	Present stimulus items without visual cue.
CLINICIAN INSTRUCTIONS:	"I'll say the name of an object, and you tell me what you do with it."
SUGGESTED CRITERIA:	90 percent accuracy without the need for additional cues, significant delays in responding, or errors of syntax and grammar.

WHAT DO YOU DO WITH (A)—
1. Rubber band.
2. Rug.
3. Button.
4. Glue.
5. Scarf.
6. Ashtray.
7. Table.
8. Scissors.
9. Tie.
10. Bandage.
11. Dictionary.
12. Detergent.
13. Alarm Clock.
14. Table Cloth.
15. Bracelet.
16. Suitcase.
17. Fireplace.
18. Ketchup.
19. Ring.
20. Paper Weight.

PHRASE PRODUCTION—*RESPONSE TO QUESTIONS*

MATERIALS:	None.
TASK INSTRUCTIONS:	Present stimulus items without visual cue.
CLINICIAN INSTRUCTIONS:	"I'll ask you a question, and you answer it with a phrase."
SUGGESTED CRITERIA:	90 percent accuracy without the need for additional cues, significant delays in responding, or errors of syntax and grammar.

WHAT WOULD YOU DO IF YOU WANTED TO—
 1. Know the meaning of a new word?
 2. See a zebra?
 3. Relax?
 4. Wash clothes?
 5. Get some sandpaper and nails?
 6. Go to Chicago?
 7. Eat gourmet food?
 8. Talk to a friend in New York?
 9. Buy a diamond ring?
10. Get a new puppy?
11. Get a driver's license?
12. Know the most recent world news?
13. Know how to make a certain dessert?
14. Know what programs are on T.V.?
15. Learn how to play the flute?
16. See a clown?
17. Put out a small fire?
18. Get rid of a guest?
19. Get a piece of furniture from the store to your house?
20. Cut some wood?

PHRASE PRODUCTION — *RESPONSE TO QUESTIONS*

MATERIALS:	None.
TASK INSTRUCTIONS:	Present stimulus items without visual cue.
CLINICIAN INSTRUCTIONS:	"I'll ask you a question, and you answer it with a phrase."
SUGGESTED CRITERIA:	90 percent accuracy without the need for additional cues, significant delays in responding, or errors of syntax and grammar.

WHAT DO YOU DO—
1. At the circus?
2. At a party?
3. At church?
4. With a plant?
5. At the zoo?
6. In a rainstorm?
7. In a den?
8. On an athletic track?
9. In a hospital?
10. In a garden?
11. At a pharmacy?
12. At a pet shop?
13. In a gym?
14. During the winter?
15. During the summer?
16. In the mountains?
17. In a cafeteria?
18. At a resort?
19. At a friend's house?
20. On a boat?

PHRASE PRODUCTION—*RESPONSE TO QUESTIONS*

MATERIALS:	None.
TASK INSTRUCTIONS:	Present stimulus items without visual cue.
CLINICIAN INSTRUCTIONS:	"I'll ask you a question, and you answer it with a phrase."
SUGGESTED CRITERIA:	90 percent accuracy without the need for additional cues, significant delays in responding, or errors of syntax and grammar.

WHAT DO YOU DO—
1. On a tennis court?
2. In a grocery store?
3. At the hardware store?
4. In a library?
5. At a music school?
6. With your relatives?
7. At a parade?
8. At a barber shop?
9. In the garage?
10. With a young child?
11. In the living room?
12. In an orchard?
13. With a hall closet?
14. On an athletic field?
15. At a bakery?
16. In a museum?
17. At a concert?
18. At the theatre?
19. With a shelf?
20. On a patio?

PHRASE PRODUCTION—*RESPONSE TO QUESTIONS*

MATERIALS: None.

TASK INSTRUCTIONS: Present stimulus items without visual cue.

CLINICIAN INSTRUCTIONS: "I'll ask you a question, and you answer it with a phrase."

SUGGESTED CRITERIA: 90 percent accuracy without the need for additional cues, significant delays in responding, or errors of syntax and grammar.

WHAT DO YOU DO WHEN—
1. You have a headache?
2. Your house is messy?
3. You find a hole in your shirt?
4. Your power goes off?
5. A wastebasket is completely full?
6. You are sick to your stomach?
7. Your pen runs out of ink?
8. A lightbulb goes out?
9. Someone starts crying?
10. The phone rings?
11. The alarm clock goes off?
12. You need a prescription refilled?
13. Your car breaks down?
14. You run out of money?
15. You have to get to the roof of your house?
16. You are locked out of your house?
17. Your T.V. is broken?
18. Your hands are cold?
19. You leave your keys in the car?
20. You put too much pepper on your eggs?

PHRASE PRODUCTION—*RESPONSE TO QUESTIONS*

MATERIALS:	None.
TASK INSTRUCTIONS:	Present stimulus items without visual cue.
CLINICIAN INSTRUCTIONS:	"I'll ask you a question, and you answer it with a phrase."
SUGGESTED CRITERIA:	90 percent accuracy without the need for additional cues, significant delays in responding, or errors of syntax and grammar.

WHAT WOULD YOU DO IF YOU—
1. Lost your glasses?
2. Broke the lead of your pencil?
3. Got a cut on your finger?
4. Saw a man lying in the street?
5. Spilled juice on your pants?
6. Lost a button?
7. Needed the phone number of a local store?
8. Were too cold?
9. Were too hot?
10. Needed a haircut?
11. Needed a loaf of bread?
12. Were tired?
13. Had trouble hearing people?
14. Had a friend in the hospital?
15. Discovered that your house had been broken into?
16. Found someone's wallet?
17. Got lost in a strange city?
18. Were given an extra thousand dollars?
19. Saw flames coming from your neighbor's window?
20. Found someone lying unconscious on the floor?

PHRASE PRODUCTION — *SENTENCE COMPLETION*

MATERIALS: None.

TASK INSTRUCTIONS: Present stimulus items without visual cue.

CLINICIAN INSTRUCTIONS: "I'll start a sentence, and you finish it with a phrase. Finish these sentences."

SUGGESTED CRITERIA: 90 percent accuracy without the need for additional cues, significant delays in responding, or errors of syntax and grammar.

1. Tomorrow we will_____.
2. Please remember to_____.
3. Every weekend I_____.
4. When I was a child I_____.
5. He had a cast on his leg because he_____.
6. At the restaurant we_____.
7. In church they_____.
8. Yesterday I_____.
9. In the store I_____.
10. At the zoo we_____.
11. In the summer we_____.
12. Every morning he_____.
13. Tonight I will_____.
14. When it's cold I_____.
15. When I'm sick I_____.
16. With two dollars he_____.
17. When the car broke down I_____.
18. Every time the bell rings I_____.
19. My finger was bleeding, so I_____.
20. When I'm too hot, I_____.

PHRASE PRODUCTION — *SENTENCE COMPLETION*

MATERIALS:	None.
TASK INSTRUCTIONS:	Present stimulus items without visual cue.
CLINICIAN INSTRUCTIONS:	"I'll start a sentence, and you finish it with a phrase. Finish these sentences."
SUGGESTED CRITERIA:	90 percent accuracy without the need for additional cues, significant delays in responding, or errors of syntax and grammar.

1. When I fell down someone_____.
2. Every night he_____.
3. When you get here, let's_____.
4. After the movie, let's_____.
5. In the library, she_____.
6. In two years, we_____.
7. When my dog was sick, I_____.
8. If it stops raining, let's_____.
9. I wish you would_____.
10. At four o'clock they_____.
11. He cut down the tree because it_____.
12. When I need more food, I_____.
13. I wrote him a letter, but he_____.
14. My watch was broken, so I_____.
15. I had a stomachache because I_____.
16. When I wanted a new saw, I_____.
17. If I get lonely, I_____.
18. When it gets dark, I_____.
19. I took the bike with me because I_____.
20. I turned off the radio, because it_____.

PHRASE PRODUCTION—*SENTENCE COMPLETION*

MATERIALS: None.

TASK INSTRUCTIONS: Present stimulus items without visual cue.

CLINICIAN INSTRUCTIONS: "I'll start a sentence, and you finish it with a phrase. Finish these sentences."

SUGGESTED CRITERIA: 90 percent accuracy without the need for additional cues, significant delays in responding, or errors of syntax and grammar.

1. After the party we_____.
2. When I'm with them we always_____.
3. When my clothes are dirty, I_____.
4. When my husband/wife is late, I_____.
5. I bruised my arm when I_____.
6. She hurried home from work because she_____.
7. I saw an old friend when I_____.
8. He cut his finger when he_____.
9. He cleaned the floor because I_____.
10. The chair broke when she_____.
11. The cat will scratch if you_____.
12. I wish I could eat it, but if I do I_____.
13. The dog barks whenever you_____.
14. The baby will smile if you_____.
15. I quit smoking because it_____.
16. We climbed to the top because we_____.
17. My mother gets angry whenever you_____.
18. I got out a map to see_____.
19. The door was locked, so I_____.
20. She turned on the light when she_____.

PHRASE PRODUCTION—*SENTENCE COMPLETION*

MATERIALS:	None.
TASK INSTRUCTIONS:	Present stimulus items without visual cue.
CLINICIAN INSTRUCTIONS:	"I'll start a sentence, and you finish it with a phrase. Finish these sentences."
SUGGESTED CRITERIA:	90 percent accuracy without the need for additional cues, significant delays in responding, or errors of syntax and grammar.

1. The fog was thick, so_____.
2. The room was hot, so_____.
3. The box was empty, so_____.
4. It was snowing hard, so_____.
5. The pen was out of ink, so_____.
6. My father hates cats, so_____.
7. The machine was still running, so_____.
8. My sister loves flowers, so_____.
9. The table was sticky, so_____.
10. He had been working hard, so_____.
11. The book was boring, so_____.
12. There was a hole in my pants, so_____.
13. The phone was busy, so_____.
14. The plant was dry, so_____.
15. The lights went out, so_____.
16. Winter is coming, so_____.
17. The plane was delayed, so_____.
18. The little boy was naughty, so_____.
19. We were going on vacation, so_____.
20. The roads were slippery, so_____.

PHRASE PRODUCTION—*SENTENCE COMPLETION*

MATERIALS: None.

TASK INSTRUCTIONS: Present stimulus items without
                         visual cue.

CLINICIAN INSTRUCTIONS: "I'll start a sentence, and you
                         finish it with a phrase. Finish
                         these sentences."

SUGGESTED CRITERIA: 90 percent accuracy without the
                         need for additional cues,
                         significant delays in responding,
                         or errors of syntax and
                         grammar.

1. It was raining, so_____.
2. I was tired, so_____.
3. I was hungry, so_____.
4. I was mad, so_____.
5. She has no money, so_____.
6. It was cold, so_____.
7. My clothes were wet, so_____.
8. I was all alone, so_____.
9. The pencil was dull, so_____.
10. The store was out of my favorite soup, so_____.
11. The squirrel came close to me, so_____.
12. The T.V. was broken, so_____.
13. The bell rang, so_____.
14. The baby was hungry, so_____.
15. It was warm outside, so_____.
16. My father was sick, so_____.
17. I was getting fat, so_____.
18. My hands were sticky, so_____.
19. The shoes were too tight, so_____.
20. My guest hated chicken, so_____.

PHRASE PRODUCTION—*SENTENCE COMPLETION*

MATERIALS:	None.
TASK INSTRUCTIONS:	Present stimulus items without visual cue.
CLINICIAN INSTRUCTIONS:	"I'll start a sentence, and you finish it with a phrase. Finish these sentences."
SUGGESTED CRITERIA:	90 percent accuracy without the need for additional cues, significant delays in responding, or errors of syntax and grammar.

1. My hands were dirty because_____.
2. The plant died because_____.
3. She slammed the door because_____.
4. I bought a new watch because_____.
5. He was in the hospital because_____.
6. I went to the hardware store because_____.
7. He ripped up the letter because_____.
8. I watered the garden because_____.
9. We turned off the T.V. because_____.
10. She built a fire because_____.
11. He got a haircut because_____.
12. She turned on the radio because_____.
13. He called the police because_____.
14. The teacher made John stay after school because_____.
15. The policeman gave him a ticket because_____.
16. We opened all the windows because_____.
17. The child hid under the bed because_____.
18. We left the party early because_____.
19. He put on his sneakers because_____.
20. They packed their suitcases because_____.

PHRASE PRODUCTION—*SENTENCE COMPLETION*

MATERIALS:	None.
TASK INSTRUCTIONS:	Present stimulus items without visual cue.
CLINICIAN INSTRUCTIONS:	"I'll start a sentence, and you finish it with a phrase. Finish these sentences."
SUGGESTED CRITERIA:	90 percent accuracy without the need for additional cues, significant delays in responding, or errors of syntax and grammar.

1. I went upstairs because_____.
2. I didn't eat dinner because_____.
3. He went home early because_____.
4. She didn't leave until late because_____.
5. I've stopped eating sweets because_____.
6. The dog barked because_____.
7. The mailman didn't come today because_____.
8. The grass was wet because_____.
9. The car wouldn't start because_____.
10. He was angry because_____.
11. We went to town because_____.
12. I took an aspirin because_____.
13. They cut down the tree because_____.
14. I had a stomachache because_____.
15. I went to work early because_____.
16. My hair was dirty because_____.
17. The child cried because_____.
18. He returned the sweater because_____.
19. The refrigerator smelled because_____.
20. My mother was happy because_____.

PHRASE PRODUCTION—*SENTENCE COMPLETION*

MATERIALS:	None.
TASK INSTRUCTIONS:	Present stimulus items without visual cue.
CLINICIAN INSTRUCTIONS:	"I'll start a sentence, and you finish it with a phrase. Finish these sentences."
SUGGESTED CRITERIA:	90 percent accuracy without the need for additional cues, significant delays in responding, or errors of syntax and grammar.

1. I will get fat if_____.
2. The toast will burn if_____.
3. The butter will melt if_____.
4. You should go to the doctor if_____.
5. The logs will not burn if_____.
6. The milk will spoil if_____.
7. You will get sick if_____.
8. The glass will break if_____.
9. You will cut your finger if_____.
10. He will get a ticket if_____.
11. You will get a cavity if_____.
12. The dog will bite me if_____.
13. You will get cold if_____.
14. The child will cry if_____.
15. The car will get a flat if_____.
16. Her leg will break if_____.
17. You will need a new pair of shoes if_____.
18. I will get drunk if_____.
19. They will lose the game if_____.
20. We will need a new car if_____.

PHRASE PRODUCTION—*SENTENCE COMPLETION*

MATERIALS: None.

TASK INSTRUCTIONS: Present stimulus items without visual cue.

CLINICIAN INSTRUCTIONS: "I'll start a sentence, and you finish it with a phrase. Finish these sentences."

SUGGESTED CRITERIA: 90 percent accuracy without the need for additional cues, significant delays in responding, or errors of syntax and grammar.

1. I will go to town if_____.
2. I will buy it if_____.
3. He will not like it if_____.
4. She will be angry if_____.
5. I will take it away if_____.
6. My father will be happy if_____.
7. We will be late if_____.
8. We won't leave if_____.
9. I can't sleep if_____.
10. We will get lost if_____.
11. He will be tired if_____.
12. The dog will bark if_____.
13. I will not come to see you if_____.
14. You should stay if_____.
15. You will ruin your new pants if_____.
16. They will call my father if_____.
17. I will put it away if_____.
18. I will punish her if_____.
19. She will get into trouble if_____.
20. They will sue the company if_____.

SENTENCE FORMULATION

SENTENCE FORMULATION—*RESPONSE TO QUESTIONS*

MATERIALS:	None.
TASK INSTRUCTIONS:	Stimulus items presented without visual cues.
CLINICIAN INSTRUCTIONS:	"I'll ask you a question, and you answer it in a complete sentence. If I ask, 'Do you wear a hat on your feet?' You say, 'No, I wear a hat on my head.' "
SUGGESTED CRITERIA:	90 percent accuracy without additional cues, significant delays in responding, or errors in syntax and grammar.

1. Do you wear socks on your hands?
2. Do you write with a watch?
3. Do birds fly in the ground?
4. Do cows give coffee?
5. Is July in the fall?
6. Do you give milk to plants?
7. Do you wear shoes on your hands?
8. Do dentists cut hair?
9. Do dogs wag their ears?
10. Does a car have three wheels?
11. Is your brother a girl?
12. Do you catch fish in a swimming pool?
13. Do you wash with a towel?
14. Do you eat soup with a knife?
15. Do flowers bloom in the winter?
16. Do stars shine during the day?
17. Do barbers repair teeth?
18. Can you drink soda through a shoestring?
19. Does candy taste sour?
20. Do you deposit money in a still?

SENTENCE FORMULATION—*RESPONSE TO QUESTIONS*

MATERIALS:	None.
TASK INSTRUCTIONS:	Stimulus items presented without visual cues.
CLINICIAN INSTRUCTIONS:	"I'll ask you a question and you answer it in a complete sentence. If I ask, 'Do you wear a hat on your feet?' You say, 'No, I wear a hat on my head.' "
SUGGESTED CRITERIA:	90 percent accuracy without additional cues, significant delays in responding, or errors in syntax and grammar.

1. Does beef come from chickens?
2. Do you have five fingers on each foot?
3. Do you write letters with a crayon?
4. Do you season soup with sugar?
5. Do you take temperatures with a calendar?
6. Do you cut meat with a spoon?
7. Can you write with a dime?
8. Do you cook food on a refrigerator?
9. Do you curl the hair on your hands?
10. Do you drink coffee from a shoe?
11. Is April a month in the summer?
12. Do men wear dresses?
13. Do you put a saddle on a tiger?
14. Do you listen to music on a radiator?
15. Do you buy food in a church?
16. Do you wear a hat on your hand?
17. Does a mailman deliver the milk?
18. Are oranges and apples tasty vegetables?
19. Do firemen put out lights?
20. Are hangers for washing clothes?

SENTENCE FORMULATION—*RESPONSE TO QUESTIONS*

MATERIALS:	None.
TASK INSTRUCTIONS:	Stimulus items presented without visual cues.
CLINICIAN INSTRUCTIONS:	"I'll ask you a question, and you answer it in a complete sentence. If I ask, 'Do you wear a hat on your feet?' You say, 'No, I wear a hat on my head.' "
SUGGESTED CRITERIA:	90 percent accuracy without additional cues, significant delays in responding, or errors in syntax and grammar.

1. Do you sleep on a floor?
2. Do you sip soda through a hose?
3. Do plumbers repair wires?
4. Do you eat ice cream for breakfast?
5. Do you enter a house through a window?
6. Do ball players play catch with a block?
7. Do you ski on sand?
8. On your finger, do you wear a tie?
9. Do policemen direct the flow of water?
10. Do you shoot arrows with a gun?
11. Do you wear a coat when it's hot?
12. Do men shave with a knife?
13. Do you swim in a tent?
14. Do you take pictures with a calendar?
15. Does pork come from cows?
16. When you're sick, do you go to a circus?
17. Do you live in a shoe?
18. Do you fly in a car?
19. Do you buy gasoline at a market?
20. Do you look up definitions in a cookbook?

SENTENCE FORMULATION—*GIVEN NOUN STIMULUS*

MATERIALS:	None.
TASK INSTRUCTIONS:	Present stimulus items without visual cue.
CLINICIAN INSTRUCTIONS:	"I'll say the name of an object, and you tell me, in a complete sentence, what you do with it."
SUGGESTED CRITERIA:	90 percent accuracy without the need for additional cues, significant delays in responding, or errors of syntax and grammar.

1. Cup
2. Money
3. Car
4. Soap
5. Book
6. Pen
7. Comb
8. Hammer
9. Chair
10. Scissors
11. Bell
12. Match
13. Bed
14. Pencil
15. Watch
16. Telephone
17. Razor
18. Kite
19. Flag
20. Belt

1. Umbrella
2. Saw
3. Broom
4. Spoon
5. Brush
6. Camera
7. Straw
8. Stamp
9. Menu
10. Radio
11. Newspaper
12. Shoes
13. Bicycle
14. Pillow
15. Rake
16. House
17. Ladder
18. Ball
19. Knife
20. Gum

SENTENCE FORMULATION—*GIVEN NOUN STIMULUS*

MATERIALS:	None.
TASK INSTRUCTIONS:	Present stimulus items without visual cue.
CLINICIAN INSTRUCTIONS:	"I'll say the name of an object, and you tell me, in a complete sentence, what you do with it."
SUGGESTED CRITERIA:	90 percent accuracy without the need for additional cues, significant delays in responding, or errors of syntax and grammar.

1. Dishes
2. Needle and thread
3. Fireplace
4. Stove
5. Dictionary
6. Elevator
7. Toothpaste
8. Scales
9. Screwdriver
10. Seeds
11. Suitcase
12. Envelope
13. Handkerchief
14. Rug
15. Tent
16. Hose
17. Garden
18. Balloon
19. Desk
20. Wallet

1. Anchor
2. Hook
3. Zipper
4. Lightbulb
5. Briefcase
6. Eraser
7. Shovel
8. Needle
9. Napkin
10. Stop sign
11. Battery
12. Log
13. Car bumper
14. String
15. Rubber band
16. Tobacco
17. Soda
18. Nail file
19. Aspirin
20. Lamb

SENTENCE FORMULATION — *GIVEN NOUN STIMULUS*

MATERIALS:	None.
TASK INSTRUCTIONS:	Present stimulus items without visual cue.
CLINICIAN INSTRUCTIONS:	"I'll say a word, and you make up a sentence using that word. Use the following words in a sentence."
SUGGESTED CRITERIA:	90 percent accuracy without the need for additional cues, significant delays in responding, or errors of syntax and grammar.

1. Sock	1. Message	1. Rainbow
2. Key	2. Folder	2. Theatre
3. Rain	3. Secret	3. Department
4. Leaves	4. Sidewalk	4. International
5. Plate	5. Plastic	5. Espionage
6. Stamp	6. Square	6. Illustration
7. Bread	7. Hole	7. Catastrophe
8. Snow	8. Gallon	8. Situation
9. Belt	9. Jacket	9. Method
10. Paper	10. Color	10. Catalog
11. Test	11. Fence	11. Charity
12. Table	12. Arrow	12. Auditorium
13. Letter	13. Pillow	13. Podium
14. Box	14. Binder	14. Monument
15. Candy	15. Floor	15. Reservation
16. Game	16. Poem	16. Reception
17. Race	17. Club	17. Statue
18. Day	18. Bakery	18. Currency
19. Home	19. Library	19. Subscription
20. Mail	20. Ink	20. Appointment

SENTENCE FORMULATION—*GIVEN VERB STIMULUS*

MATERIALS: None.

TASK INSTRUCTIONS: Present stimulus items without visual cue.

CLINICIAN INSTRUCTIONS: "I'll say a word, and you make up a sentence using that word. Use the following words in a sentence."

SUGGESTED CRITERIA: 90 percent accuracy without the need for additional cues, significant delays in responding, or errors of syntax and grammar.

1. Eat	1. Discover	1. Save
2. Sit	2. Rub	2. Clap
3. Read	3. Squeeze	3. Empty
4. Drink	4. Cry	4. Slice
5. Walk	5. Frown	5. Construct
6. Chew	6. Tickle	6. Conclude
7. Climb	7. Retire	7. Measure
8. Run	8. Recline	8. Participate
9. Draw	9. Elevate	9. Cultivate
10. Write	10. Depress	10. Illustrate
11. Talk	11. Remove	11. Describe
12. Pound	12. Deliver	12. Report
13. Wash	13. Tie	13. Prepare
14. Listen	14. Carve	14. Recite
15. Cook	15. Borrow	15. Punish
16. Sweep	16. Light	16. Arrange
17. Drive	17. Brush	17. Organize
18. Throw	18. Taste	18. Entertain
19. Dig	19. Chop	19. Encourage
20. Laugh	20. Swim	20. Divide

SENTENCE FORMULATION—*GIVEN ADJECTIVE STIMULUS*

MATERIALS:	None.
TASK INSTRUCTIONS:	Present stimulus items without visual cue.
CLINICIAN INSTRUCTIONS:	"I'll say a word, and you make up a sentence using that word. Use the following words in a sentence."
SUGGESTED CRITERIA:	90 percent accuracy without the need for additional cues, significant delays in responding, or errors of syntax and grammar.

1. Pretty		1. Noisy
2. Broken		2. Kind
3. Dirty		3. Sweet
4. Big		4. Sour
5. Funny		5. Simple
6. Small		6. Sad
7. Round		7. Happy
8. Soft		8. Busy
9. Hard		9. Tired
10. Fast		10. Naughty
11. Slow		11. Pleasant
12. Warm		12. Messy
13. Hot		13. Cute
14. Cool		14. Angry
15. Cold		15. Spicy
16. Fat		16. Rusty
17. Warm		17. Ragged
18. Thin		18. Clever
19. Nice		19. Careless
20. Comfortable		20. Little

SENTENCE FORMULATION—*GIVEN FUNCTOR WORD STIMULUS*

MATERIALS: None.

TASK INSTRUCTIONS: Present stimulus items without
                       visual cue.

CLINICIAN INSTRUCTIONS: "I'll say a word, and you make
                       up a sentence using that word.
                       Use the following words in a
                       sentence."

SUGGESTED CRITERIA: 90 percent accuracy without the
                       need for additional cues,
                       significant delays in responding,
                       or errors of syntax and
                       grammar.

1. If	1. Or	1. Away
2. As	2. Can	2. When
3. Not	3. May	3. Back
4. At	4. On	4. Never
5. Ago	5. After	5. That
6. On	6. Before	6. The
7. She	7. Front	7. An
8. My	8. Beside	8. A
9. He	9. Shall	9. Should
10. It	10. Must	10. Could
11. To	11. Will	11. Over
12. For	12. Is	12. In
13. Of	13. This	13. I
14. They	14. Those	14. Maybe
15. Them	15. Us	15. But
16. There	16. Him	16. Because
17. Then	17. Her	17. Though
18. Too	18. Just	18. Does
19. By	19. While	19. Did
20. With	20. Where	20. And

SENTENCE FORMULATION—*GIVEN PHRASE STIMULUS*

MATERIALS:	None.
TASK INSTRUCTIONS:	Present stimulus items without visual cue.
CLINICIAN INSTRUCTIONS:	"I'll say a phrase, and you make up a sentence using each phrase. Make up a sentence using the following phrases."
SUGGESTED CRITERIA:	90 percent accuracy without the need for additional cues, significant delays in responding, or errors of syntax and grammar.

1. On and on
2. Because of the accident
3. Over the hill
4. Down the street
5. If it snows
6. In a while
7. From now on
8. At the front
9. On the ground
10. For a nap
11. In the kitchen
12. Stick of gum
13. Glass of milk
14. Roll of stamps
15. At the party
16. In your pocket
17. Because of you
18. If you like
19. With some help
20. In the garage

SENTENCE FORMULATION—*GIVEN PHRASE STIMULUS*

MATERIALS: None.

TASK INSTRUCTIONS: Present stimulus items without visual cue.

CLINICIAN INSTRUCTIONS: "I'll say a phrase, and you make up a sentence using each phrase. Make up a sentence using the following phrases."

SUGGESTED CRITERIA: 90 percent accuracy without the need for additional cues, significant delays in responding, or errors of syntax and grammar.

1. Into the corner
2. Like to
3. Around the corner
4. In the meantime
5. With a smile
6. In black and white
7. For an hour
8. A while ago
9. For a walk
10. To the bank
11. In a second
12. After the movie
13. If it rains
14. Before the game
15. Up and down
16. Cats and dogs
17. Up the steps
18. Down the mountain
19. Over the fence
20. By the way

SENTENCE FORMULATION—*GIVEN PHRASE STIMULUS*

MATERIALS:	None.
TASK INSTRUCTIONS:	Present stimulus items without visual cue.
CLINICIAN INSTRUCTIONS:	"I'll say a phrase, and you make up a sentence using each phrase. Make up a sentence using the following phrases."
SUGGESTED CRITERIA:	90 percent accuracy without the need for additional cues, significant delays in responding, or errors of syntax and grammar.

1. Because of the weather
2. With a dime
3. In the store
4. If they can
5. But I can't
6. Because of the heat
7. When we go
8. With some help
9. A gallon of
10. A package of
11. A piece of
12. In the corner
13. On the table
14. If you can
15. In the sink
16. In the closet
17. Young and old
18. Whenever you can
19. As soon as possible
20. As fast as

SENTENCE FORMULATION—*GIVEN TWO UNRELATED WORDS*

MATERIALS: None.

TASK INSTRUCTIONS: Present stimulus items without visual cue.

CLINICIAN INSTRUCTIONS: "I'll say two words, and you make up a sentence using both words in the sentence. Use the following words in a sentence."

SUGGESTED CRITERIA: 90 percent accuracy without the need for additional cues, significant delays in responding, or errors of syntax and grammar.

1. Angry—plant
2. He—his
3. Early—ill
4. There—fish
5. Today—if
6. She—her
7. I—my
8. They—their
9. All—family
10. Hurry—friends
11. From—oven
12. On—his
13. Do—didn't
14. Pair—had
15. Enjoy—both
16. Some—she
17. Did—out
18. Early—maybe
19. Straight—water
20. Wish—because

SENTENCE FORMULATION—*GIVEN TWO UNRELATED WORDS*

MATERIALS:	None.
TASK INSTRUCTIONS:	Present stimulus items without visual cue.
CLINICIAN INSTRUCTIONS:	"I'll say two words, and you make up a sentence using both words in the sentence. Use the following words in a sentence."
SUGGESTED CRITERIA:	90 percent accuracy without the need for additional cues, significant delays in responding, or errors of syntax and grammar.

1. Will—where
2. For—who
3. Will—dozen
4. Lots—hungry
5. House—ready
6. School—after
7. When—able
8. Sweater—until
9. Tall—airplane
10. Jump—pencil
11. How—that
12. Bird—laugh
13. Believe—belt
14. Tight—floor
15. Hair—sink
16. Two—lake
17. Grass—crazy
18. Fly—float
19. Peel—tired
20. Soft—happy

SENTENCE FORMULATION—*GIVEN TWO UNRELATED WORDS*

MATERIALS:	None.
TASK INSTRUCTIONS:	Present stimulus items without visual cue.
CLINICIAN INSTRUCTIONS:	"I'll say two words, and you make up a sentence using both words in the sentence. Use the following words in a sentence."
SUGGESTED CRITERIA:	90 percent accuracy without the need for additional cues, significant delays in responding, or errors of syntax and grammar.

1. To—while
2. With—much
3. But—won't
4. May—give
5. For—such
6. Get—when
7. Do—for
8. How—like
9. What—this
10. Will—that
11. If—can
12. Because—there
13. Only—in
14. Pair—to
15. Your—that
16. Until—gone
17. Far—back
18. From —good
19. Dirty—go
20. Those—up

SENTENCE FORMULATION—*QUESTION PRODUCTION*

MATERIALS:	None.
TASK INSTRUCTIONS:	Present stimulus items without visual cue.
CLINICIAN INSTRUCTIONS:	"I'll say a phrase, and you make up a question beginning with that phrase."
SUGGESTED CRITERIA:	90 percent accuracy without the need for additional cues, significant delays in responding, or errors of syntax and grammar.

1. Who was
2. What do
3. When does
4. Where can
5. Why do
6. How much
7. How many
8. How often
9. How soon
10. Can you
11. May I
12. Which one
13. Do they
14. Will you
15. Could I
16. Should they
17. Does he
18. What if
19. Is she
20. Have you

SENTENCE FORMULATION—*QUESTION PRODUCTION*

MATERIALS:	None.
TASK INSTRUCTIONS:	Present stimulus items without visual cue.
CLINICIAN INSTRUCTIONS:	"I'll say a word, and you make up a question beginning with each word."
SUGGESTED CRITERIA:	90 percent accuracy without the need for additional cues, significant delays in responding, or errors of syntax and grammar.

1. Who
2. What
3. When
4. Where
5. Why
6. How
7. Will
8. Can
9. May
10. Do
11. Is
12. Which
13. Could
14. Have
15. Can't
16. Won't
17. Wasn't
18. Shouldn't
19. Wouldn't
20. If

SENTENCE FORMULATION—*GIVEN INTRODUCTORY SENTENCE*

MATERIALS:	None.
TASK INSTRUCTIONS:	Present stimulus without visual cue.
CLINICIAN INSTRUCTIONS:	"I'm going to say a sentence, then you make up a sentence to follow it. For instance, if I say, 'It was a hot summer day,' you might add, 'My friends and I went to the beach.'"
SUGGESTED CRITERIA:	90 percent accuracy without the need for additional cues, significant delays in responding, or errors of syntax and grammar.

1. It was a cold winter day.
2. My neighbor went on vacation.
3. She woke up with a sore throat.
4. The water at the lake was very cold.
5. It was Saturday Morning.
6. I woke up because I heard a loud noise.
7. The traffic was terrible that night.
8. The store was very crowded.
9. He was quite hard of hearing.
10. He was sitting in the corner chair.
11. The cat had scratched up all the good furniture.
12. The child had been sick all day.
13. I got up and had a big breakfast.
14. The sun was shining brightly.
15. We leave on vacation in one week.
16. The dessert tasted terrible, but my wife/husband had cooked it.
17. The airplane landed on time.
18. He went outside and started mowing the lawn.
19. Tomorrow my cousin is coming to town.
20. The book was boring.

SENTENCE FORMULATION—*GIVEN INTRODUCTORY SENTENCE*

MATERIALS:

None.

TASK INSTRUCTIONS:

Present stimulus without visual cue.

CLINICIAN INSTRUCTIONS:

"I'm going to say a sentence, then you make up a sentence to follow it. For instance, if I say, 'It was a hot summer day,' you might add, 'My friends and I went to the beach.' "

SUGGESTED CRITERIA:

90 percent accuracy without the need for additional cues, significant delays in responding, or errors of syntax and grammar.

1. She spilled the coffee on her husband's silk tie.
2. I couldn't see the cars because of the thick fog.
3. He fell off his bicycle.
4. The train was delayed for two hours.
5. The man was angry because no one came to serve him.
6. The restaurant on the corner has the best food in town.
7. My car ran out of gas.
8. I was having trouble finding my wallet.
9. She was nervous about meeting the new boss.
10. He bumped into the police car accidently.
11. After she put her coat on, she left the house.
12. During the rainstorm the children had to stay indoors.
13. There was not enough room in the car for the suitcases.
14. My mother loves to buy expensive dresses.
15. The man ran 4 miles to the beach.
16. Before we left, I called my brother.
17. Because of her injury, she could not play tennis.
18. After the game, they watched a good movie.
19. When I'm sad, I go for a walk to the lake.
20. He couldn't understand why his son was angry.

SENTENCE FORMULATION— *UNSCRAMBLING A SENTENCE*

MATERIALS: None.

TASK INSTRUCTIONS: Present stimulus items without visual cue.

CLINICIAN INSTRUCTIONS: "I'll read you a sentence with the word order mixed up. I want you to unscramble the sentence and tell me what the sentence really is. Unscramble these sentences."

SUGGESTED CRITERIA: 90 percent accuracy without the need for additional cues, significant delays in responding, or errors of syntax and grammar.

1. Locked door front the is
2. Button was coat the missing a
3. To I want dinner eat
4. Bread I baked loaf of a
5. New a they house bought
6. On they married were Saturday
7. Was watch the broken
8. Game to I the went
9. Studied dinner I before
10. Letter the put mailbox in the I
11. Camping the went boy scouts on trip a
12. Tire bicycle has the flat a
13. Directed policeman the traffic the
14. Dollar I may borrow a
15. Eat it time to is dinner
16. Party he birthday went a to
17. Started September on school twenty-first
18. Water too was the hot
19. Car traveling was the fast too
20. Out burning fire of the was control

SENTENCE FORMULATION—*UNSCRAMBLING SENTENCES*

MATERIALS:	None.
TASK INSTRUCTIONS:	Present stimulus items without visual cue.
CLINICIAN INSTRUCTIONS:	"I'll read you a sentence with the word order mixed up. I want you to unscramble the sentence and tell me what the sentence really is. Unscramble these sentences."
SUGGESTED CRITERIA:	90 percent accuracy without the need for additional cues, significant delays in responding, or errors of syntax and grammar.

 1. Ran car gas of the out
 2. Hole sock my it in has a
 3. Of glass may have I water a
 4. School after home right come
 5. Door at someone front is the
 6. The movie children to went a
 7. Had bicycle a tire the flat
 8. Tree blew the down a storm
 9. The emptied janitor the trash
10. Dentist my the tooth filled
11. Was account my overdrawn checking
12. Down lines were telephone blown the
13. The sun hot ice cream the melted
14. The bee was child stung a by
15. Order out alarm was the fire of
16. Married the radiant his groom bride
17. Puppy the garden the destroyed flower
18. With mountains covered the were snow
19. The worked two days on mechanic the for car
20. Nail child rusty a stepped the on

SENTENCE FORMULATION — *UNSCRAMBLING SENTENCES*

MATERIALS:	None.
TASK INSTRUCTIONS:	Present stimulus items without visual cue.
CLINICIAN INSTRUCTIONS:	"I'll read you a sentence with the word order mixed up. I want you to unscramble the sentence and tell me what the sentence really is. Unscramble these sentences."
SUGGESTED CRITERIA:	90 percent accuracy without the need for additional cues, significant delays in responding, or errors of syntax and grammar.

1. Cup would of like coffee a I
2. Car the gas out ran of
3. Dishes in dirty are sink the kitchen the
4. Better breakfast I felt after
5. Lawn the rains mow before it
6. Letter mail time the when have the you
7. Table an hour we for waited our
8. Order called meeting the to director the
9. Agreement fighters made an between was the
10. Ten broken was watch slow minutes
11. Announced governor the policies new state the
12. Jury the presented the attorney his to case
13. Seasoned salt was soup and the pepper with
14. Prescribed the medication doctor the necessary
15. Destroyed because the of drought crop was the
16. Angry her was because died plant she had
17. Contained the numerous documents valuable envelope
18. Poor was tip the so service waitress I not the did
19. At crowd angry the yelled referee the
20. Influenced American by the economy is gross product national the

COMPLEX SENTENCE FORMULATION

DESCRIPTION OF OBJECTS

MATERIALS: None.

TASK INSTRUCTIONS: Stimulus items presented
                            without visual cues.

CLINICIAN INSTRUCTIONS: "I'll say the name of an object,
                            and you describe it in terms of
                            shape, color, size, material
                            composition, and function."

SUGGESTED CRITERIA: 90 percent accuracy without
                            additional cues, significant
                            delays in responding, or errors
                            of syntax and grammar.

TELL ME ABOUT A—
 1. Table
 2. Refrigerator.
 3. Banana.
 4. Can.
 5. Scissors.
 6. Desk.
 7. Train.
 8. Blotter.
 9. Cannon.
10. Pencil sharpener.
11. Log.
12. Paper clip.
13. Fence.
14. Sofa.
15. Rug.
16. Wheel barrow.
17. Watering can.
18. Grocery cart.
19. Calendar.
20. Tape recorder.

DESCRIPTION OF ANIMALS AND PEOPLE

MATERIALS:	None.
TASK INSTRUCTIONS:	Stimulus items presented without visual cues.
CLINICIAN INSTRUCTIONS:	"I'll say the name of a person or an animal, and you describe it in terms of function, appearance, size, and location."
SUGGESTED CRITERIA:	90 percent accuracy without additional cues, significant delays in responding, or errors in syntax and grammar.

TELL ME ABOUT A—
1. Bee
2. Zebra
3. Bear
4. Lion
5. Elephant
6. Mouse
7. Penguin
8. Peacock
9. Snail
10. Snake
11. Fireman
12. Policeman
13. Nurse
14. Doctor
15. Football player
16. Ballerina
17. Clown
18. Waitress
19. Your mother
20. Your father

DESCRIPTION OF PLACES

MATERIALS: None.

TASK INSTRUCTIONS: Stimulus items presented without visual cues.

CLINICIAN INSTRUCTIONS: "I'll say the name of a place, and you describe it in terms of appearance, function, and size."

SUGGESTED CRITERIA: 90 percent accuracy without additional cues, significant delays in responding, or errors in syntax and grammar.

TELL ME ABOUT A—
1. Park
2. Grocery store
3. School
4. Gas Station
5. Hospital
6. Patio/Porch
7. Cafeteria
8. Living room
9. Utility room
10. Country Club
11. Circus
12. Hardware store
13. Library
14. Jungle
15. Beach
16. Kitchen
17. Zoo
18. Museum
19. Prison
20. Gym

ANSWERING "WHY" QUESTIONS

MATERIALS: None.

TASK INSTRUCTIONS: Stimulus items presented without visual cues.

CLINICIAN INSTRUCTIONS: "I'll ask you a question, and you answer it with a complete sentence."

SUGGESTED CRITERIA: 90 percent accuracy without additional cues, significant delays in responding, or errors in syntax and grammar.

1. Why do we brush our teeth?
2. Why do some women wear makeup?
3. Why do we put meat in the refrigerator?
4. Why do razor blades have to be sharp?
5. Why do we eat soup out of a spoon rather than a fork?
6. Why do spiders make webs?
7. Why do we use water with soap?
8. Why does a baby suck his thumb instead of his toe?
9. Why do men wear neckties sometimes?
10. Why do we put salt on some of our food?
11. Why do most people work?
12. Why do we use umbrellas?
13. Why do we sleep?
14. Why do we take off our clothes before we take a shower?
15. Why don't children drive?
16. Why do teachers need blackboards?
17. Why do windows have shades?
18. Why are children told not to touch things in stores?
19. Why do some people get divorced?
20. Why are anchors made of heavy iron?

ANSWERING "WHY" QUESTIONS

MATERIALS:	None.
TASK INSTRUCTIONS:	Stimulus items presented without visual cues.
CLINICIAN INSTRUCTIONS:	"I'll ask you a question, and you answer it with a complete sentence."
SUGGESTED CRITERIA:	90 percent accuracy without additional cues, significant delays in responding, or errors in syntax and grammar.

1. Why do we wear belts?
2. Why do we have teeth?
3. Why do we wear boots in the rain?
4. Why do we wear watches?
5. Why do babies cry?
6. Why do we wear coats outside?
7. Why do construction workers wear hard hats?
8. Why do we have gardens?
9. Why do we wear shoes?
10. Why do firemen need water?
11. Why do postmen need mail trucks?
12. Why do policemen carry guns?
13. Why do we avoid snakes?
14. Why do children go to school?
15. Why do pencils have erasers?
16. Why do kitchens have sinks?
17. Why do some people wear hats?
18. Why do some people wear glasses?
19. Why do gardeners need shovels?
20. Why do some women wear high heels?

ANSWERING "WHY" QUESTIONS

MATERIALS: None.

TASK INSTRUCTIONS: Stimulus items presented
                            without visual cues.

CLINICIAN INSTRUCTIONS: "I'll ask you a question, and you
                            answer it with a complete
                            sentence."

SUGGESTED CRITERIA: 90 percent accuracy without
                            additional cues, significant
                            delays in responding, or errors
                            in syntax and grammar.

1. Why do robbers wear masks?
2. Why are windows made of glass?
3. Why do fifty-year-old men gain weight more easily than
   sixteen-year-old boys?
4. Why are fingernails useful?
5. Why do some men wear mustaches?
6. Why do we have fingers? (Instead of one large palm?)
7. Why don't pens have white ink in them?
8. Why do children shout less while eating than while playing?
9. Why do we use a salt shaker instead of a soup spoon to put
   salt on our eggs?
10. Why do children wear masks on Halloween?
11. Why do we use potholders?
12. Why do some people give parties?
13. Why don't pens have erasers?
14. Why do lamps have shades?
15. Why do most dogs wear collars?
16. Why do we drink coffee out of a cup instead of a glass?
17. Why do you jack up a car to change a tire?
18. Why do states require doctors to be licensed?
19. Why do we drink soup out of a bowl instead of a plate?
20. Why can't an exercise bicycle go anywhere?

DESCRIPTION OF LIKENESSES AND DIFFERENCES

MATERIALS: None.

TASK INSTRUCTIONS: Stimulus items presented
                               without visual cues.

CLINICIAN INSTRUCTIONS: "I'll say two words, and you tell
                               me how they are alike and
                               different."

SUGGESTED CRITERIA: 90 percent accuracy without
                               additional cues, significant
                               delays in responding, or errors
                               in syntax and grammar.

WHAT ARE THE DIFFERENCES AND SIMILARITIES
    BETWEEN (A)—
1. Pen and pencil.
2. Cat and dog.
3. House and barn.
4. Water and milk.
5. Watch and clock.
6. Mittens and gloves.
7. Broom and mop.
8. Couch and chair.
9. Airplane and bird.
10. Nickle and dime.
11. Rain and snow.
12. Cup and glass.
13. Sun and moon.
14. Flashlight and lamp.
15. Motorcycle and bicycle.
16. Shoes and boots.
17. Skirt and dress.
18. Supper and dinner.
19. Bedspread and blanket.
20. Globe and map.

DESCRIPTION OF LIKENESSES AND DIFFERENCES

MATERIALS: None.

TASK INSTRUCTIONS: Stimulus items presented without visual cues.

CLINICIAN INSTRUCTIONS: "I'll say two words, and you tell me how they are alike and different."

SUGGESTED CRITERIA: 90 percent accuracy without additional cues, significant delays in responding, or errors in syntax and grammar.

WHAT ARE THE DIFFERENCES AND SIMILARITIES BETWEEN (A)—

1. Jam and honey.
2. Sailboat and canoe.
3. Hot dog and hamburger.
4. River and lake.
5. Ball and balloon.
6. Tree and bush.
7. Newspaper and magazine.
8. Box and drawer.
9. Wig and toupee.
10. Boots and rubbers.
11. French fries and mashed potatoes.
12. Spoon and shovel.
13. Table and chair.
14. Bike tire and car tire.
15. Socks and stockings.
16. Horse and pony.
17. Plate and bowl.
18. Stool and chair.
19. Teeth and fangs.
20. T.V. and radio.

DESCRIPTION OF LIKENESSES AND DIFFERENCES

MATERIALS: None.

TASK INSTRUCTIONS: Stimulus items presented without visual cues.

CLINICIAN INSTRUCTIONS: "I'll say two words, and you tell me how they are alike and different."

SUGGESTED CRITERIA: 90 percent accuracy without additional cues, significant delays in responding, or errors in syntax and grammar.

WHAT ARE THE DIFFERENCES AND SIMILARITIES BETWEEN (A)—

1. Curtains and window shades.
2. Cigar and cigarette.
3. Baseball and basketball.
4. Igloo and tent.
5. Cafeteria and restaurant.
6. Check and dollar bill.
7. Trunk and suitcase.
8. Doctor and nurse.
9. Farm and zoo.
10. Story and article.
11. Material and cloth.
12. Picture and painting.
13. Breakfast and lunch.
14. Fountain pen and ballpoint pen.
15. Feet and paws.
16. Ice and snow.
17. Eyeglasses and binoculars.
18. Sidewalk and street.
19. Window and door.
20. Commercials and advertisements.

EXPLANATION OF EXPRESSIONS

MATERIALS: None.

TASK INSTRUCTIONS: Stimulus items presented
                          without visual cues.

CLINICIAN INSTRUCTIONS: "I'll say a common expression,
                          and you tell me what it means."

SUGGESTED CRITERIA: 90 percent accuracy without
                          additional cues, significant
                          delays in responding, or errors
                          in syntax and grammar.

1. Don't cry over spilt milk.
2. Better to be safe than sorry.
3. Haste makes waste.
4. Life is not a bed of roses.
5. I'm over the hill.
6. Look before you leap.
7. Too many cooks spoil the broth.
8. Turn over a new leaf.
9. Birds of a feather flock together.
10. He's a card!
11. Keep your fingers crossed.
12. You've got something up your sleeve.
13. It never rains but it pours.
14. He's smelling like a rose.
15. A tightwad.
16. He drives me up a wall!
18. There's more than one way to skin a cat.
18. There are many more fish in the sea.
19. You only reap what you sew.
20. When push comes to shove.

EXPLANATION OF EXPRESSIONS

MATERIALS:	None.
TASK INSTRUCTIONS:	Stimulus items presented without visual cues.
CLINICIAN INSTRUCTIONS:	"I'll say a common expression, and you tell me what it means."
SUGGESTED CRITERIA:	90 percent accuracy without additional cues, significant delays in responding, or errors in syntax and grammar.

1. By the skin of his teeth.
2. He's a glutton for punishment.
3. It's not my cup of tea.
4. It's raining cats and dogs.
5. A stitch in time saves nine.
6. A bird in the hand is worth two in the bush.
7. He who hesitates is lost.
8. Out of sight, out of mind.
9. Silence is golden.
10. All that glitters is not gold.
11. All work and no play makes jack a dull boy.
12. You're pulling my leg.
13. He bit the dust.
14. Don't look a gift horse in the mouth.
15. He lives in a pig's sty.
16. It's six of one and one-half dozen of another.
17. I'm caught between a rock and a hard spot.
18. Up the creek without a paddle.
19. You can't get blood out of a turnip.
20. It's like talking to a wall.

DEFINITIONS

MATERIALS:	None.
TASK INSTRUCTIONS:	Stimulus items presented without visual cues.
CLINICIAN INSTRUCTIONS:	"I'll say a word, and you tell me what it means. Define the following words."
SUGGESTED CRITERIA:	90 percent accuracy without additional cues, significant delays in responding, or errors in syntax and grammar.

1. Remove
2. Tomorrow
3. Vacation
4. Interview
5. Aunt
6. Cousin
7. Parade
8. Include
9. Opinion
10. Frequent
11. Dependent
12. Vacant
13. Time
14. Job
15. Emergency
16. Instructions
17. Occupied
18. Guest
19. Reservation
20. Adventure

DEFINITIONS

MATERIALS: None.

TASK INSTRUCTIONS: Stimulus items presented without visual cues.

CLINICIAN INSTRUCTIONS: "I'll say a word, and you tell me what it means. Define the following words."

SUGGESTED CRITERIA: 90 percent accuracy without additional cues, significant delays in responding, or errors in syntax and grammar.

1. Certain
2. Teach
3. Discount
4. Entertainment
5. Interrogate
6. Tempting
7. Transportation
8. Requirement
9. Modern
10. Unusual
11. Empty
12. Bitter
13. Investigate
14. Award
15. Peaceful
16. Security
17. Popular
18. Destroy
19. Invent
20. Lend

MULTIPLE SENTENCE AND PHRASE FORMULATION

MATERIALS:	None.
TASK INSTRUCTIONS:	Stimulus items presented without visual cues.
CLINICIAN INSTRUCTIONS:	"I'm going to ask you some questions, and you answer them using more than one sentence or phrase."
SUGGESTED CRITERIA:	90 percent accuracy without additional cues, significant delays in responding, or errors in syntax and grammar.

WHAT ARE SOME OF THE—
 1. Ways to use a tin can?
 2. Things you might need a box for?
 3. Things people do in the summer?
 4. Ways to use a paper bag?
 5. Reasons for cutting down trees?
 6. Reasons lines of people form?
 7. Reasons babies cry?
 8. Things that make you cold?
 9. Reasons crowds form?
10. Things you need to do to prepare for a vacation?
11. Things you can do with a piece of string?
12. Reasons people take pills?
13. Ways to use a notebook?
14. Ways in which we use our fingernails?
15. Reasons to give parties?
16. Some of the things you do to prepare for winter?
17. Reasons for turning on the radio?
18. Reasons people are in a hospital?
19. Reasons people may be late?
20. Ways to use an elastic band?

MULTIPLE SENTENCE AND PHRASE FORMULATION

MATERIALS:	None.
TASK INSTRUCTIONS:	Stimulus items presented without visual cues.
CLINICIAN INSTRUCTIONS:	"I'm going to ask you some questions, and you answer them using more than one sentence or phrase."
SUGGESTED CRITERIA:	90 percent accuracy without additional cues, significant delays in responding, or errors in syntax and grammar.

WHAT ARE SOME OF THE—
1. Things you can do on a vacation?
2. Things people do to break the law?
3. Things that may go wrong with a car?
4. Things you may need a knife for?
5. Information you would find in a newspaper?
6. Ways in which people use water?
7. Reasons for moving from one town to another?
8. Reasons for taking a bus instead of a car?
9. Reasons to build a fire in the forest?
10. Things you might do with a thousand dollars?
11. Things you can do with eggs?
12. Reasons to own a dog?
13. Ways to use a paper towel?
14. Reasons for needing to know the time?
15. Things to do at a lake?
16. Things that policemen do?
17. Reasons to have a rug?
18. Things you can do with a piece of bread?
19. Reasons to call people on the phone?
20. Things you can do with a key?

PARAGRAPH FORMULATION

PARAGRAPH FORMULATION

MATERIALS:	None.
TASK INSTRUCTIONS:	Stimulus items presented without visual cues.
CLINICIAN INSTRUCTIONS:	"I'll state an activity, and you tell me all the steps involved in performing it."
SUGGESTED CRITERIA:	90 percent accuracy without additional cues, significant delays in responding, or errors in syntax and grammar.

WHAT ARE ALL THE STEPS YOU TAKE IN—
1. Making toast?
2. Building a fire?
3. Washing dishes?
4. Making chocolate milk?
5. Changing a tire?
6. Getting a tan?
7. Making a jelly sandwich?
8. Planning and going on vacation?
9. Getting from your house to the grocery store?
10. Making popcorn?
11. Shampooing your hair?
12. Making tea/coffee?
13. Washing a car?
14. Taking a picture?
15. Smoking a cigarette?
16. Changing a diaper?
17. Mowing a lawn?
18. Painting a house?
19. Planning a party?
20. Raking leaves?

PARAGRAPH FORMULATION

MATERIALS: None.

TASK INSTRUCTIONS: Stimulus items presented
                             without visual cues.

CLINICIAN INSTRUCTIONS: "I'll state an activity, and you
                             tell me all the steps involved in
                             performing it."

SUGGESTED CRITERIA: 90 percent accuracy without
                             additional cues, significant
                             delays in responding, or errors
                             in syntax and grammar.

WHAT ARE ALL THE STEPS YOU TAKE IN—
 1. Setting the table?
 2. Buying shoes?
 3. Getting gasoline?
 4. Ordering in a restaurant?
 5. Shaving?
 6. Making a bed?
 7. Making a salad?
 8. Doing laundry?
 9. Planting a garden?
10. Planning a picnic?
11. Entertaining a child?
12. Buying a house?
13. Planting a lawn?
14. Polishing shoes?
15. Mailing a package?
16. Writing a letter?
17. Washing windows?
18. Buying a car?
19. Calling long distance?
20. Brushing teeth?

RETELLING A PARAGRAPH

MATERIALS:	None.
TASK INSTRUCTIONS:	Clinician reads the story to the patient without visual cues.
CLINICIAN INSTRUCTIONS:	"I'm going to read you a story, and you will listen. When I have finished, you will tell me about the story."

The Origin of the Cat

The cat ran wild for many millennia after the dog had become man's willing servant. There are no drawings of cats in prehistoric paintings. Not until around 2000 B.C. did the cat appear in written and pictorial records.

RETELLING A PARAGRAPH

MATERIALS: None.

TASK INSTRUCTIONS: Clinician reads the story to the patient without visual cues.

CLINICIAN INSTRUCTIONS: "I'm going to read you a story, and you will listen. When I have finished, you will tell me about the story."

Invention of the Bikini

The bikini was first presented at a Paris fashion show on July 5, 1946 four days after the American detonation on Bikini Atoll. Both events caused international repercussions, and thus "bikini" was coined to reflect the concept of "the ultimate." The first bikini was cotton, printed with a newspaper design.

RETELLING A PARAGRAPH

MATERIALS:	None.
TASK INSTRUCTIONS:	Clinician reads the story to the patient without visual cues.
CLINICIAN INSTRUCTIONS:	"I'm going to read you a story, and you will listen. When I have finished, you will tell me about the story."

The Statue that Got Married

In the gardens of Smitherfield stands the statue of a young woman wearing a solid gold wedding ring. The ring was found by market superintendent in 1924, and when no one claimed it, he had it soldered onto her finger. Since 1873, she had been standing there supposedly to represent fertility. He thought it was high time that she got married.

RETELLING A PARAGRAPH

MATERIALS:	None.
TASK INSTRUCTIONS:	Clinician reads the story to the patient without visual cues.
CLINICIAN INSTRUCTIONS:	"I'm going to read you a story, and you will listen. When I have finished, you will tell me about the story."

Pulitzer Capsule

In 1956 a sealed copper box was recovered during demolition of the Pulitzer Building in New York City. The box had been buried in October, 1889. Inside were the following: plans for the building, copies of New York's newspapers, a photograph of Pulitzer, some gold and silver coins, photographs of the Pulitzer family, and a commemorative medallion.

RETELLING A PARAGRAPH

MATERIALS:	None.
TASK INSTRUCTIONS:	Clinician reads the story to the patient without visual cues.
CLINICIAN INSTRUCTIONS:	"I'm going to read you a story, and you will listen. When I have finished, you will tell me about the story."

"Ann's Birthday Flowers"

After William had fallen in love with Ann, he was very thoughtful of her in every way. Ann knew he loved her, and she reminded him that this coming Wednesday was her twenty-fourth birthday. William told her that he would send her a rose for each year of her life.

When he arrived home that night, he wrote the florist for two dozen roses to be delivered to Ann on Wednesday morning. The florist was so delighted to have the order from Mr. Smith, that he put in another dozen roses for good measure.

When Ann opened the box, she could not understand why she had received three dozen roses. She was so angry that she would not speak to William for a whole week.

SUGGESTED READINGS AND MATERIALS

Brookshire, R. H.: *An Introduction to Aphasia*. BRK Publishers, 4825 Tenth Avenue South, Minneapolis, Minnesota, 1974.

Brookshire, R. H. (Ed.): *Clinical Aphasiology*. Collected Proceedings 1972-78. BRK Publishers, 4825 Tenth Avenue South, Minneapolis, Minnesota, 1978.

Eisenson, T.: *Adult Aphasia*, Assessment and Treatment. Appleton-Century-Crofts, New York, 1973.

Johns, D. F.: *Clinical Management of Neurogenic Communicative Disorders*. Little, Brown and Co., Boston, Massachusetts, 1970.

Keith, R. L.: *Speech and Language Rehabilitation: A Workbook for the Neurologically Impaired*. The Interstate Printers and Publishers, Inc., Danville, Illinois, 1972.

Kilpatrick, K., and Jones, C.: *Therapy Guide for the Adult with Language and Speech Disorders*. Visiting Nurse Service of Summit County, 1200 McArthur Drive, Akron, Ohio, 1977.

Schuell, H: *Aphasia Theory and Therapy*. University Park Press, Baltimore, Maryland, 1974.

APPENDIX

INSTRUCTIONS FOR THE ILLUSTRATIONS

The following thirty illustrations are divided into three separate groups. Each group is indicated by the letter A, B, or C; the A pictures represent words of high frequency in the English language, the B pictures represent those of medium frequency, and the C pictures are those of low frequency. Several treatment tasks throughout the manual require the use of these illustrations.

In order to use the illustrations, the clinician should remove them from the book and apply them individually to illustration board or any such material. This will enable the clinician to manipulate the cards for treatment as well as provide protection for the illustrations.

A

A

A

A

A

A

A

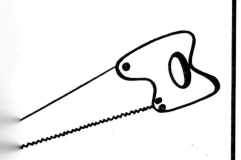

B

E

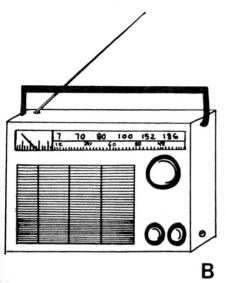

B

E

B

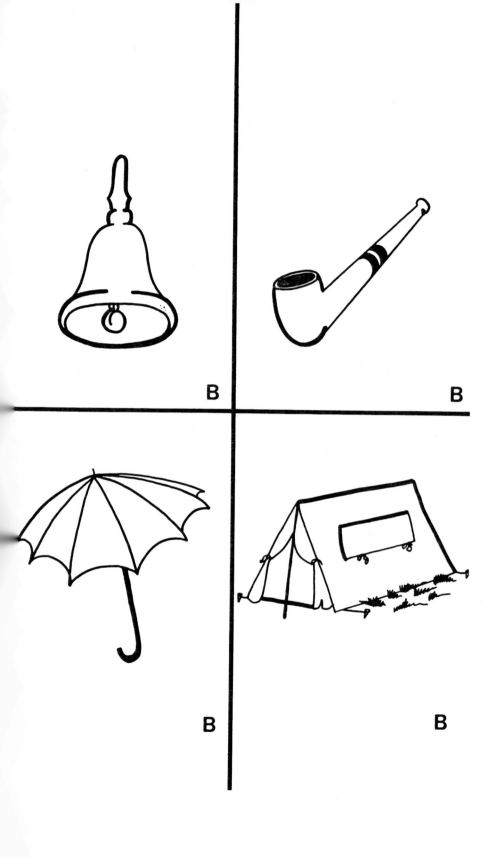

B

B

B

B

C

1980 MAY 1980

S	M	T	W	TH	F	S
					1	2	3
4	5	6	7	8	9	10
11	12	13	14	15	16	17
18	19	20	21	22	23	24
25	26	27	28	29	30	31

C

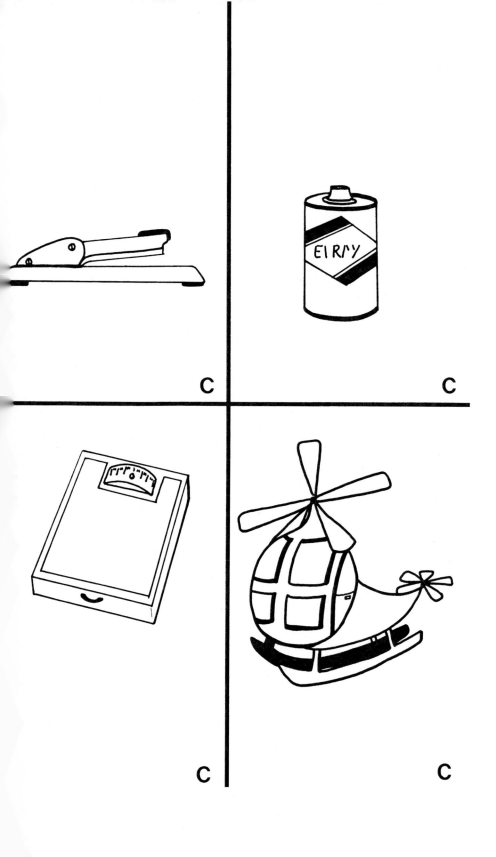

C

C

C

C

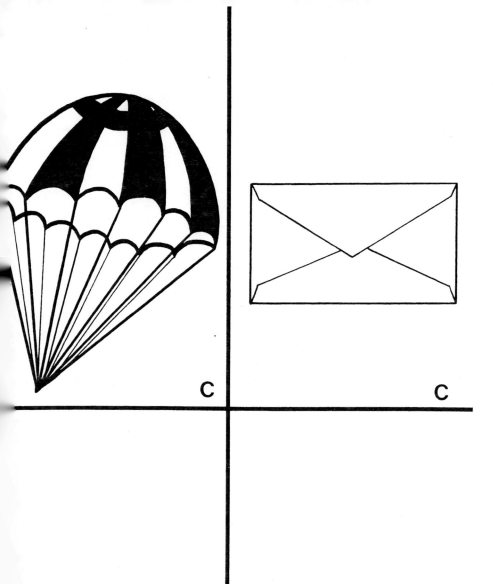

C   C

SCORE SHEET INSTRUCTIONS

The score sheet was designed for the clinician's use. It enables the clinician to document the patient's response behaviors.

It further enables the clinician to denote individual page numbers and the date of treatment for daily tallying. Use of this score sheet may assist the clinician in establishing treatment goals or determining progression in the task hierarchy.

SCORE SHEET

NAME _____

GE DATE	AUDITORY PROCESSING					VERBAL EXPRESSION				
1										
2										
3										
4										
5										
6										
7										
8										
9										
10										
11										
12										
13										
14										
15										
16										
17										
18										
19										
20